The Complete Ketogenic Diet Cookbook for Beginners

Learn the Essentials to Living the Keto Lifestyle – Lose Weight, Regain Energy, and Heal Your Body

Table of Contents

Introduction

I would like to thank you for purchasing this book, *'The Complete Ketogenic Diet Cookbook for Beginners – Learn the Essentials to Living the Keto Lifestyle – Lose Weight, Regain Energy, and Heal Your Body.'*

This book will provide you with all the information that you will need about the ketogenic diet. Following the Keto diet will help you in attaining your weight loss and fitness goals. A little bit of effort is all it takes to stick to this diet. Dieting has never been this easy! A few lifestyle changes can go a long way while following this diet. You will see a positive change in your body within the first week of following this diet.

The Keto diet is based on a simple concept. There's a high intake of naturally fatty food and low or even no intake of carbohydrates. You will learn about the Keto diet, the various benefits it has to offer as well as a list of foods that are keto friendly. I have also included tips for when you are dining out and have added some common FAQs so that your questions will be answered.

The Ketogenic diet requires you to make a few changes to your daily eating habits. The keto-friendly recipes that have been presented in this book will make the transition to the Ketogenic diet quite easy. You will simply need to plan your meals ahead so that it gets easier to follow this diet. The recipes mentioned in this book are not only easy to follow, but they will also help you to cook yummy and healthy food. All the recipes have been segregated into different categories like breakfast, appetizers, meats, and so on for the convenience of the reader. Now, all that you need to do is read this book thoroughly and put in some effort for achieving your goals.

All the best!

Chapter 1: What Is the Ketogenic Diet

The Ketogenic diet is popularly known as the Keto diet. It is a low carb and a high-fat diet. The ketones that are produced by the liver are used as the primary source of energy and hence the name of this diet. When you consume carbs, they are broken down into glucose by insulin. Insulin is a hormone that is secreted by the pancreas. The body tends to opt for glucose over other sources of energy since this is the most easily convertible one. Insulin helps in processing the glucose that is present in the blood stream. Glucose is the primary fuel when the diet mainly consists of carbohydrates. This means that all the fat is simply being stored in the cells. When your intake of carbohydrates has been reduced, your body will be induced into ketosis. Ketosis is the process where the body shifts from burning glucose to burning fats for providing energy. When your body shifts to survival mode due to a decrease in the intake of food, Ketosis naturally occurs in the body. Ketones are used as the main source of energy.

The aim of the Ketogenic diet is to induce the body into a state of ketosis. This is achieved by reducing the intake of carbohydrates. When the intake of fat increases and carbs decreases, in such a case, ketones are automatically burnt for providing energy. You should know the following about ketogenic diet.

It is designed to induce ketosis: As mentioned, the Ketogenic diet has been designed to induce the body into a state of ketosis. This is done by reducing the intake of carbs. Carbs are the usual source or energy and when their supply is cut off, then fats are burnt.

Fat is the primary source of fuel: In a Ketogenic diet, about 70% of your calorie requirement is from fat, 25% from proteins, and 5% from carbohydrates. Carbs are broken down into glucose and these are stored in the muscles and liver, whereas all the fat molecules are broken down into triglycerides and this results in adipose or fatty tissue (body fat). You will need to make sure that you are consuming sufficient fat to keep up your energy levels.

Carbohydrate cheats: Since Ketogenic diet is a low carb diet, this means that you will need to restrict your intake of carbs. Most of us are used to consuming carbs daily. In fact, a major portion of our meals is made up of carbs. So, you will need to make use of substitutes for carbs. It is as simple as that. For instance, the next time you are making spaghetti Bolognese or stir-fried noodles make use of zucchini ribbons instead of pasta or noodles. You will most certainly not miss pasta! You can substitute wheat flour with almond flour for making pasta!

This diet is a high fat and a low carb diet. You needn't worry about your cholesterol level shooting up. You will need to understand that there are two types of cholesterol; good and bad. This diet helps in increasing the levels of your good cholesterol while reducing the levels of your bad cholesterol. You will need to give your body some time to get acclimatized to the ketogenic diet. The transition isn't difficult, it just takes a while, that's all. It is advisable that you keep your exercising schedule a little light during the first ten days of this diet.

Chapter 2: Going Ketosis- How Can It Benefit you?

Reduction in your appetite:

Hunger is perhaps the most difficult side effect that you will have to cope with while on a diet. This also happens to be the leading reason why a lot of people tend to just give up on their diets. One of the advantages of a low carb diet is that it reduces your appetite. When you reduce the amount of carbs that you consume and replace them with fat and protein, the number of calories you are consuming will reduce as well.

Facilitates in weight loss:

One of the easiest and most effective ways in which you can shed all those extra kilos is by simply cutting down on the carbs that you are consuming. Studies prove that people on a low-carb diet tend to lose weight rapidly when compared to other diets. One of the main reasons for this is because the excess water that's present in your system is removed. Once the insulin levels secreted by the pancreas have reduced, the kidneys will also start getting rid of all the excess sodium and this leads to the shedding of water weight.

Most of the fat that is shed is from the abdominal region:

All the fat that's present in your body isn't the same. Depending upon the location and the concentration of fat, the health risks that are involved would also vary. The fat content in the body is usually distributed into two parts. The layer of fat under the skin and visceral fat or abdominal fat. The fat that gets accumulated around the organs is referred to as visceral fat. When the content of visceral fat is high, it not only obstructs the movement of insulin but also causes inflammation. This is considered to be a leading cause of metabolism dysfunction. A diet that's low in carbohydrates is extremely helpful in getting rid of this harmful fat. Most of the fat that's lost on the Ketogenic diet is from the abdominal cavity.

Reduction of triglycerides:

Particular kinds of fat molecules that are present in the body are referred to as triglycerides. When you observe an overnight fast, the level of triglycerides in the blood increases and this, in turn, increases the risk of various heart diseases. The consumption of carbohydrates and fructose, in particular, are responsible for causing a spike in these fat molecules.

Improvement in the level of good cholesterol:

HDL stands for High-Density Lipoprotein and it is referred to as good cholesterol. Technically it would be incorrect to call this cholesterol, as it's a lipoprotein that is responsible for carrying cholesterol molecules. There's nothing actually called good or bad cholesterol per se because all the molecules of cholesterol have the same composition. HDL and LDL are two lipoproteins that are responsible for carrying cholesterol in the bloodstream. HDL is responsible for transporting the molecules of cholesterol away from the body. The higher the level of HDL, the lower the risk of heart disease. One of the most effective ways in which you can increase your good cholesterol would be by consuming foods that are rich in fats and low in carbohydrates.

Reduction in the level of both insulin and blood sugar:

All the carbohydrates that you consume are broken down into simple sugars during digestion. When this happens, the simple sugars are free to enter the bloodstream and this leads to an increase in the level of your blood sugar. A high level of blood sugar is toxic and the body starts releasing a hormone called as insulin. Insulin helps in breaking down these simple sugars to glucose and transports these to different cells. The cells then burn this glucose for generating energy. When an individual is healthy, a spike in the blood sugar is counteracted by the production of insulin and there's no damage.

Blood pressure reduces

Hypertension is a condition where the old pressure levels are unusually high. This is a leading cause of numerous heart disease and other conditions like kidney failure. Hypertension affects all the major organs of the body and it can even cause damage to the eyesight. The Ketogenic diet has been proven to be helpful in controlling the blood pressure levels and therefore it also reduces the risk of all the above-mentioned disorders.

The level of LDL cholesterol improves

LDL refers to Low-Density Lipoprotein and it is often referred to as bad cholesterol. LDL is a lipoprotein that is responsible for transporting cholesterol molecules in the body. Research shows that individuals who have a higher level of LDL are more susceptible to heart disease. It is also important to identify the type of LDL that is present. The type of LDL is determined according to the size of the molecules. The smaller the particles, the higher the risks are of an individual of being prone to various heart diseases and vice versa.

Helps in treating several disorders of the brain

The human brain does need a constant supply of glucose. A part of the brain needs glucose to function. This is the reason why the liver produces glucose even while consuming fats instead of carbohydrates. A major part of the brain makes use of ketones and the body produces ketones during ketosis. Cutting down on the consumption of carbs can help in inducing the body into ketosis. This is the mechanism that the Ketogenic diet makes use of and it has proven to be successful in treating epilepsy to some extent, especially in children who haven't responded to any medical treatments. In the recent past, all those diets that favor a low carbohydrate consumption have been gaining popularity for helping patients with various mental disorders like Alzheimer's and Parkinson's and for coping with various symptoms of these diseases. Following the Keto diet is quite beneficial for your overall wellbeing.

Chapter 3: Foods to Avoid and Foods to Eat

You might be wondering what you should and shouldn't eat while following this diet. This chapter will provide you with a list of things that are and aren't keto friendly.

Eat Freely

Protein:
- Grass-fed meats (beef, lamb, goat, and venison)
- Fish caught in the wild
- Pastured pork, poultry, and eggs
- Gelatin
- Offal (as long as its grass fed)

Healthy fats:
- Saturated fats like lard, tallow, chicken, duck, or goose fat, ghee, butter, and coconut oil.
- Monounsaturated fats like avocado, macadamia, and olive oil
- Polyunsaturated fats derived from animal sources like fatty fish and other seafood rich in Omega-3

Non-starchy vegetables:
- Spinach, Lettuce, chives, radicchio, bok choy, and all sorts of green leafy vegetables
- Cruciferous vegetables like kale, kohlrabi, and radish
- Asparagus, cucumbers, zucchini, spaghetti squash, bamboo shoots, and celery

Beverages and condiments:
- Water, black coffee, green tea, black tea, or any other herbal teas
- (You can add a little bit of cream or coconut milk to your coffee)
- Use pork rinds for breading
- Bone broth (not the pre-packaged ones)
- Mayonnaise
- Pesto
- Mustard
- Pickles and fermented foods (like kimchi and Kombucha)
- Sauerkraut (provided you are making it at home)
- All spices and herbs are allowed
- Whey proteins without any additives, sweeteners, and hormones

Eat occasionally

Vegetables and fruits:
- Cruciferous vegetables like white and red cabbage, cauliflower, broccoli, fennel, turnips, swede, and Brussels sprouts
- Eggplants, tomatoes, peppers and other nightshades
- Couple of root vegetables like spring onions, parsley root, garlic, mushrooms, pumpkin, and leeks
- Nori, okra, sugar snap peas, bean sprouts, wax beans, water chestnuts, and artichokes
- Berries like cranberries, blackberries, blueberries, raspberries, strawberries, and so on.

Dairy products
- Full fat cream, yogurt, sour cream, cottage cheese
- (Steer clear of all those products that are labeled as "low-fat" or "diet". Most of these products have a high sugar and starch content)
- Bacon (but be vary of any added preservatives and starch)

Nuts and seeds:
- Macadamia nuts (these are rich in Omega-3 and hardly contain any carbs)
- Pecans, almonds, walnuts, sunflower seeds, pine nuts, flaxseeds, pumpkin seeds, sesame seeds, and hemp seeds
- Brazil nuts (however, they have a very high level of selenium. So, don't eat too many of those)
- Fermented soy products:
- All non-GMO and soy products like tempeh, soy sauce and other Paleo friendly soy products. Edamame and unprocessed black soybeans.

Condiments:
- Tomato products without any added sugars like puree or ketchup
- Healthy sweeteners like stevia, swerve, erythritol, and so on
- Thickeners like arrowroot powder and xanthan gum.
- Extra dark chocolate (more than 70% cocoa content and avoid soy lecithin)
- Cocoa powder and carob powder are allowed in moderation
- Steer clear of any sugar-free mints and chewing gums since they have carbs in them.
- Vegetables, fruits, nuts and seeds with average carbs (consumption would depend on your daily carbohydrate limit):

- Root vegetables (celery root, carrots, beets, parsnip, and sweet potatoes)
- Melons (watermelons, honeydew melon, and cantaloupe)
- Nuts (pistachios, cashew nuts, and chestnuts)
- Note: Apricots, dragon fruit, peaches, nectarines, apples, grapefruits, kiwis, oranges, plums, cherries, pears, and figs (better to avoid them completely, if not consume them in very small quantities)

Alcohol

- Dry red and white wines, unsweetened spirits (avoid these completely if you want to lose weight or for maintaining your weight)

Foods to avoid

➢ All grains should be avoided. Even whole meal grains like wheat, rye, corn, barley, millets, sorghum, rice, buckwheat, and other grains should be avoided. You cannot have quinoa or white potatoes. This means all products made from one or more of these grains should be completely avoided. No pasta, bread, pizzas, and so on. You can make use of alternative flours like almond flour and use them for making pasta.

➢ Pork and fish that has been farmed in factories should be avoided. These products are rich in Omega-6 fatty acids and the fish so farmed have a high content of mercury.

➢ Stay away from all sugary and sweet treats. Processed and packaged foods are rich in sugars and carbs. This means no soft drinks, ice creams, sugary syrups, and cakes.

➢ Processed foods that contain carrageenan (like products containing almond milk), products that contain MSG, dried fruits (that contain sulfites), and wheat glutens.

➢ Stay away from artificial sweeteners like Splenda, Equal, and other sweeteners containing saccharin, sucralose, and aspartame.

➢ Refined fats, oils, and trans fats like margarine aren't allowed. You cannot use sunflower oil, cottonseed oil, canola oil, corn oil, grapeseed oil, and even soybean oil.

➢ Stay away from all sorts of products that are labeled as low fat, low carb, zero carb and diet. These contain artificial additives that aren't good for your health.

➢ Milk is allowed as long as it is full fat. Milk is usually not recommended for different reasons. Milk is the most difficult to digest when compared to all the other dairy products. Pasteurized milk doesn't have any good bacteria in it and it could even contain hormones. The carb content of milk is quite high. A small amount of milk is fine for your daily coffee or tea. However, don't forget to keep an eye on all the carbs you are consuming.

➢ Stay away from alcoholic drinks and other sweet drinks. Added sugars won't do your body any good while on a diet.

- ➤ Tropical fruits like pineapple, mangoes, papayas, and bananas aren't allowed. There are a few fruits that have a high carb count like tangerine and grapes. Avoid consuming any fruit juices, even the ones that say they are 100% natural. Juices contain additives and added sugars. This isn't good for your health. Smoothies are a better option and they have more fiber content in them.
- ➤ Avoid soy products for various health reasons apart from a few products that are non-GMO fermented. Avoid wheat gluten that's used in low-carb food products. Products containing MSG aren't permitted as well.

Chapter 4: Ketogenic Diet FAQ

How long does it take for ketosis to set in?

A keto diet isn't one that you can keep going on and off. It will take your body some time to get adjusted and for ketosis to set in. This process could take anywhere between two to seven days. It is dependent on the level of activity, your body type and the food that you are eating. If you start exercising on an empty stomach, this will help in inducing ketosis rather quickly. Start restricting your carb consumption to less than 20g per day and be mindful of the amount of water that you are consuming.

What about low carb recipes?

All the recipes that you need have been provided in this book! You needn't worry about having to search for low carb recipes. The recipes provided in this book have been divided into different categories for the convenience of the reader. So, you have got recipes for different courses. Once you get a hang of all the things you can and cannot eat, you can start experimenting on your own. All that you will need to do will be to plan your meals in advance.

How to track the intake of carbs?

There are various mobile applications that you can make use of for tracking your carbohydrate intake. There are paid and free applications as well. These apps will help you in keeping a track of your total carbohydrate and fiber intake. However, you won't be able to track your net carb intake. MyFitnessPal is one of the popular apps. You just need to open the app store on your smartphone and you can select an app from the various apps that are available.

Is it necessary to count calories?

Calories do matter. There are different reasons that you will need to be mindful of while counting calories. You will need to eat properly and make sure that your body doesn't have a severe deficit of calories. Also, don't indulge in snacks that aren't good for you. While on a keto diet, you don't usually have to worry about the calories you are consuming due to all the fats and proteins that you will be consuming for filling yourself up. If you exercise regularly, then make sure that you have consumed sufficient calories and that your body isn't experiencing a huge calorie deficit.

What about eating too much of fat?

To state it simply, you can eat fat. Your body will need to be in a state of the caloric deficit for losing weight. This means that calories are an important marker at the end of the day. If you start consuming too much fat, then this will turn the caloric deficit into a surplus. It isn't easy to overeat while on a low carb and a high-fat diet like keto, but it is still possible. Make use of apps for keeping track of your macros and check the amount of fats, proteins and carbs you should be consuming.

What would the weight loss be like?

The amount of weight that you will lose will depend on you. If you add exercise to your daily routine, then the weight loss will be greater. If you cut down on foods that stall weight loss, then this will speed up the process. For instance, completely cutting out things like artificial sweeteners, dairy and wheat products and other related products will definitely help in speeding up your weight loss. During the first two weeks of the keto diet, you will end up losing all the excess water weight. Ketosis has a diuretic effect on the body and you might end up losing a couple of pounds within the first few days of this diet. After this, your body will adapt itself to burning fats for generating energy, instead of carbs.

How can you tell if your body is in ketosis?

The most common way in which you can tell whether your body is in ketosis or not is by making use of Ketostix. These can be found in any local pharmacy. However, you should keep in mind that they can be quite inaccurate. Usually, they will give you an idea whether ketosis has been induced or not. If the stick turns purple or pink, this shows that your body is producing ketones. If it is a darker color, then this could mean that you are dehydrated and that the levels of ketone in your urine are quite concentrated. Ketostix will help in measuring the levels of acetone present in your urine. Ketones when unused produces acetone. The Ketostix help in measuring the acetone present in your urine and these are the unused ketones present. The ketones that are made use of by your brain and body for generating energy are known as Beta-Hydroxybutryate (BHB) and the Ketostix doesn't measure these. If you want an accurate measure of the ketone levels in your body, then you should make use of a blood ketone meter. These will show you the actual number of ketones present in the bloodstream and aren't easily influence by hydration or the lack of it. If you have got a blood ketone meter, then the readings would be:

> ➤ Light ketosis would be between 0.5 – 0.8mmol/L
> ➤ Medium ketosis would be between 0.9- 1.4mmol/L
> ➤ Deep ketosis would be between 1.5-3.0mmol/L (for best weight loss).

How does Ketosis work?

To put it simply, Ketosis is the state that the body would be induced into when you don't consume any carbohydrates. The body will start making use of fats for providing energy. So, fats including the body fats would be the primary source of fuel. It not only healthier, but it is also a more efficient source of fuel for the brain. You might be wondering how energy is generated from all the fats present. Well, in the state of Ketosis, the liver helps in breaking down the fat molecules and produces ketones. These ketones are made use of for providing the necessary energy. How does all this help in losing weight? When there is a deficit of calories, the body starts making use of the stored reserves of fat for providing the energy it needs. The human body has been designed in such a manner that they have reserves of fat, in case our food intake decreases. These fat reserves are hardly ever made use of and lead to weight gain. Reducing the calorie intake by cutting down on carbs helps in losing their extra kilos.

Should you worry about all the fat that you are consuming?

The fats that we consume can be categorized into three main groups and these are saturated fats, polyunsaturated fats, and monounsaturated fats. It was a general misconception that saturated fats were bad for health. However, these fats help in improving your level of cholesterol. So, you needn't worry about these fats. The tricky part would be dealing with polyunsaturated fats. There are two things that you need to be aware of while dealing with polyunsaturated fats. Things like margarine and vegetable oils consist of polyunsaturated fats and they have trans-fat in it. You should strictly stay away from this. However, when these polyunsaturated fats are present naturally in foods (like in fish), then they are good for your health and will improve your overall level of cholesterol as well. Then there are monounsaturated fats. These fats are considered to be healthy. Olive oil would be the best example of these fats and they help in reducing your overall level of cholesterol as well.

What are Macros and how can you count them?

Macro is the term that is usually used for macronutrients. The three main macronutrients are fats, proteins and carbs. As mentioned earlier, calories don't really matter. However, it would be better if you kept track of these at the beginning. It will enable you to see how you are doing on the diet. You will truly be surprised about the amount of carbs that we end up consuming unknowingly. If you have come to a standstill in your weight loss, then tracking macros will be helpful. You will be able to pinpoint at the different things in your diet that might be causing this. You will start thinking in terms of grams when you start tracking your macros. You shouldn't think in terms of % but think in terms of grams. For instance, a lot of people think that 75% fat, 20% protein, and 5% carbs are good. However, that's not the case. Grams will help you in getting an accurate description of what you are eating. You needn't worry if you are off by a bit on your macros; it really isn't a big deal. There is a wiggle room for about 10-15 grams of fats as well as proteins in most cases. You needn't worry if you go a little over or a little under on some days. If you are keeping track of your calories and it isn't too much in deficit, then you are doing fine.

What can be done if you feel a little low during the initial phase of the diet?

During the initial phase of the keto diet, you might experience mild headaches and feel a little low on energy as well. Ketosis has a diuretic effect on the body and this results in an increase in the urge to urinate more than usual. Added to this, your body is burning up the glycogen stores, and you have got a minor problem on your hands. The electrolytes are being pushed out of your body. So, you will need to replace them. Keep yourself fully hydrated. Add a little salt to your food. Consume plenty of broths, and have lots of water. The transition into ketosis will be quite simple and you can make it easy on yourself by staying hydrated.

What can be done if you experience constipation?

Your bowel movements might undergo a change while starting out on keto. You might or might not experience constipation. Here are a few things that you can do for restoring normalcy to your bowel movements. Add in a magnesium supplement, drink lots of water, a tbsp. of coconut oil will help, in case you eat nuts then stop doing so for a while, consume fibrous vegetables, chia or flax seeds would help, and you can try some coffee or some tea.

Is alcohol permitted?

You can consume alcohol while on the ketogenic diet. However, be mindful of the amount of alcohol you consume. Alcohol is a really good source of carbs to creep into your diet. You should concentrate on the liquor you are drinking. Wine, beer, and different cocktails have carbs in them. So, clear liquor would be a safe bet. However, stay away from all sorts of flavored liquors since they have got carbs in them as well.

What can be done if you stop losing weight?

You might have reached a standstill in your weight loss. There are a lot of reasons that could contribute to this. You can do a couple of things for resuming your weight loss. Cut down a few things from your diet or you could change your eating pattern as well. Here are a few suggestions that you can make use of. You can try any of the following strategies. You can cut down on dairy, increase your fat intake, decrease the intake of carbs, stop consuming nuts, cut out gluten, no artificial sweeteners, watch out for additional carbs, cut down on processed foods and switch to measuring yourself instead of weighing yourself.

What about working out?

People who exercise can be broadly categorized into those who run and those who lift weights. If you like cardio (running, biking, and the like) then you don't have to worry. It is different when it comes to lifting weights though. Carbs do help in your performance and they help with the recovery of muscle as well. This means faster grains and better performance during your training sessions. There are two options you have and these are TKD and CKD. TKD stands for targeted keto diet. In this, you will consume sufficient carbs prior to your workout so that your body is temporarily displaced from ketosis for the duration of the workout and you have got sufficient supply of glycogen. Once you have burned all of this up, then your body will return to the state of ketosis. CKD stands for cyclical ketogenic diet. It is an advanced technique. You shouldn't make use of it if you are just getting started with the keto diet. This is usually for bodybuilding and for competitors who would want to stay in ketosis while building their muscle. In this, you will stay on a regular keto diet and then do a carb-up for two days (usually over the weekend). In this method, you are simply helping your body in replenishing the glycogen stores for the training that you will need to do for the rest of the week. Your aim would be to extinguish these glycogen stores before they can be replenished once again.

Chapter 5: Tips for Eating Out

Have you started the Keto diet? Well, that's wonderful. Are you going out for a meal tonight? You needn't worry about that. You can go out and eat out, provided you keep a few things in mind. A low-carb diet can work anywhere and here are a few tips that will help you in making your diet work.

Eliminating all the starch:

Pass on the bread, avoid pasta, stay away from potatoes, and say no to rice. Keep the temptation away from your plate and order for something without any starch. If you are ordering an entrée, then you can substitute the starchy side with a salad or some extra vegetables. If the restaurant has a provision for it, then you can get them to substitute a lettuce wrap for the bread in a sandwich or a burger. If it cannot be substituted, then simply leave that item. You can also explain your dietary restrictions to your server and get them to prepare something without any starchy items. The meals served at restaurants might be low in fat and this would make it seem like it is important to eat carbs for feeling full. However, this has a simple solution. You can ask for some extra butter on your veggies, some additional dressing with oil for your salad. Make sure that you check with your server the oil they are using. Ask them for some olive oil instead of the regular vegetable oil that they might be serving with their food.

The condiments matter as well

There are some sauces like the Béarnaise that are mostly fatty. Then there are things like the barbecue sauce and ketchup that are rich in carbs. Gravies can go either way. If you aren't sure of the sauce, then you can ask for its ingredients and see whether or not it has flour or sugar in it. Alternatively, you can ask for the sauce on the side and then you can decide whether you would want to add it to your meal or not.

Choose your drink carefully

The perfect option for drinks would be water (sparkling or still), tea or coffee. If you want to have some alcoholic beverage, then opt for champagne, dry wine or spirits. Be mindful of the quantity, those carbs can creep in at any time.

Dessert

If you find that you are still hungry, then you can indulge in a cup of tea or coffee while the rest can finish their sweet treats. Good options would be decaf coffee or herbal tea as well. Stay away from desserts. A good option would be berries and some heavy cream. Or add in some cream to your coffee for satiating your sweet tooth.

Get a little creative

If you feel that there is nothing on the menu that would work for you, then you can improvise a little. Perhaps you can go for spaghetti Bolognese sans the spaghetti. You could ask your server to get you a portion of the sauce in a bowl with a side of vegetables. Add a little bit of Parmesan to it and it would be tasty on its own. Or you could odder an appetizer. You can order a salad and pair it with some shrimp cocktail or even a plate of cheese. This will be a good low-carb dinner for you. You are the customer, you can ask them for suggestions.

At a buffet restaurant

When you go for a buffet, there are plenty of options to choose from. There would certainly be a few low-carb dishes to choose from. You don't have to eat your money's worth. You should eat for your health and you should enjoy your meal. Before you leave your table to take in the spread offered, set a few ground rules for yourself, like skipping everything that is starchy. This will include all grains, pasta, potatoes and sugar in any form. You should pick up a small plate. You can always go back for more. Shift your focus to healthy foods like the salad bar, platters of veggies and even seafood options available. You can always add a few healthy fats to it like olive oil, sour cream, butter, and even some cheese. You can always ask your server to bring you these to your table if you couldn't find them at the buffet. Always take your time to enjoy your meal. Eat your food slowly and chew on it deliberately. You certainly don't have to rush for more and don't stuff yourself with food.

A friend or a relative's place

You needn't worry about attending a dinner party or going for a holiday gathering. Your hosts will be pretty considerate of your needs and food preferences. You can perhaps inform your host about your preference for low-carb foods so that they can accommodate your needs. Before going to the party, you can fill yourself up on a fatty keto-friendly snack at home. This will take the edge off your hunger and it would be easier for you to resist starchy foods. You need to remember that this is just one meal. You can give yourself a cheat day and indulge in some regular food. However, be mindful of the amount of carbs you are eating. Pass on the breadbasket, but maybe you can have some fried chicken! It would be recommended that you don't give into your sweet cravings. Have a cup of coffee instead. You can also call your host ahead and probably get a low-carb dish along with you. This will help you in sticking to your diet without having to trouble your host.

Fast food restaurants

At a deli or a bakery, you can opt for a salad with a fatty dressing. You can include all the low-carb foods that you want to in it, like chicken, shrimp, cheese, eggs, olives, lettuce, and so on. Add plenty of dressing to your salad.

There will be plenty of options to choose from. You can load up on toppings and avoid as much of the crust as possible. You should opt for anything that is low-carb and has a high-fat content. Going out needn't be a pain and you shouldn't have to worry about it. You needn't shy away from any social commitments. All that you will need to do will be to plan a little ahead and you will be fine. The alternative would be to munch on a low carb snack before heading out. This will help in sticking to the diet without any difficulty.

Chapter 6: Ketogenic Breakfast Recipes
Cream Cheese Pancakes

Serves: 4

Ingredients

- 55 grams cream cheese
- 2 large eggs
- 1 tbsp. sugar substitute
- 1 tbsp. rolled oats
- ½ tsp. cinnamon
- Some strawberries for garnish

Method

1. In a large bowl, beat some cream cheese using a spoon or an electric beater until it is nice and fluffy.
2. Now crack the eggs, one by one and beat the mixture again.
3. Lightly crush the oats using a pounder.
4. Drizzle some sugar substitute, cinnamon powder and gently fold it in.
5. Grease a saucepan with some oil or butter and heat it over medium flame.
6. Add one scoop of batter and gently spread it across the pan. Cook the pancake for about 2 minutes until they turn golden brown. Now flip it over and cook for another minute. Repeat the process for the remaining batter.
7. Transfer to a large dish.
8. Roughly chop some strawberries and add them on top of the pancakes.
9. Serve warm.

Mocha Chia Pudding

Serves: 2

Ingredients

- 2 tbsp. dark coffee
- 80 ml chia seeds
- 80 ml coconut cream
- 1 tbsp. vanilla extract
- 1 tbsp. swerve
- 2 tbsp. cacao nibs
- 480 ml cups water

Method

1. Boil about 80 ml of water in a large vessel over medium heat. Add the coffee powder and boil for another 15 minutes until the liquid is reduced to half.
2. Strain the coffee using a strainer and blend in the coconut cream and swerve. You can use a blender to slightly whisk the mixture.
3. Now add the cacao nibs, chia seeds and let the mixture cool down for about 30 minutes.
4. Add some vanilla extract to the mixture and blend it well using a spoon.
5. You can add some more coffee powder and transfer the mixture into small ramekins.
6. Refrigerate for about 30 minutes and serve chilled.

Keto Waffles

Serves: 2

Ingredients

- 5 whole eggs
- 4 tbsp. coconut flour
- 3 tbsp. sugar substitute
- ¼ tsp. baking soda
- 4 tbsp. chocolate shavings
- 1 tbsp. coconut flour

Method

1. In a large bowl, add some flour, baking soda and mix well using a spoon.
2. In another bowl, crack the eggs and beat them using a fork. Add some vanilla essence and mix well again.
3. Now pour the liquid ingredients to the other bowl and whisk again.
4. Heat the waffle maker over medium flame.
5. Pour about one scoop of batter on the waffle maker and cook for 5 minutes on each side until slightly golden brown.
6. Transfer the waffles on a large plate, sprinkle some chocolate shavings on top and serve warm.
7. You can also serve a scoop of vanilla ice cream to go with it.

*Note: You can also use half cup of oats instead of coconut flour. Just make sure that you pound them gently using a pounder and blend it in the remaining mixture.

Baked Spiced Granola

Serves: 4

Ingredients

- 110 grams pecans, chopped
- 55 grams walnuts, chopped
- 55 grams almonds, slivered
- 55 grams coconut flakes, unsweetened
- 55 grams almond meal
- 28 grams flax meal
- 28 grams pepitas
- 28 grams sunflower seeds
- 60 ml melted butter
- 55 grams sugar substitute
- 1 tbsp. honey
- 1 tsp. cinnamon powder
- 1 tsp. vanilla
- ½ tsp. nutmeg
- ½ tsp. salt
- 80 ml water

Method

1. Preheat the oven to 170 C.
2. In a large bowl, combine all the nuts with flax meal, pepitas, sunflower seeds, sugar substitute, honey, ground cinnamon, nutmeg, salt, almond meal, coconut flakes and mix well using a spoon.
3. Drizzle some melted butter on top along with some almond meal and gently fold it in.
4. Place a parchment paper on a baking tray.
5. Transfer the granola tray and place another sheet of parchment paper on the granola. Now firm it using a rolling pin and even it out.
6. Place the tray in the oven and bake it for up to 90 minutes until brown and crisp. Let it cool off for about 30 minutes and store in an airtight container.
7. You can mix some granola with chilled almond milk and eat it for breakfast.

Flourless Cottage Cheese and Egg Muffins

Serves: about 12 muffins

Ingredients

- 55 grams almond meal
- 55 grams hemp seeds
- 55 grams parmesan cheese, grated
- 28 grams flax seed meal
- 28 grams nutritional yeast
- ½ tsp. baking powder
- ½ tsp. spike seasoning
- ¼ tsp. salt
- 6 large eggs
- 55 grams cottage cheese
- 35 grams green onions, sliced

Method

1. Preheat the oven to 190 C.
2. Grease the muffin cups using a cooking spray.
3. In a large bowl, combine almond meal, hemp seeds, cheese, flax seed meal, yeast flakes, baking powder, spike seasoning, salt and mix well using a large spoon.
4. In another bowl, crack the eggs and beat them lightly using a fork. Add grated cheese, some chopped green onion and whisk.
5. Now pour this mixture into the flour mixture and whish lightly using a beater. Make sure that you don't overbeat the mixture.
6. Pour this batter into the muffin molds until they are nearly full.
7. Place the molds on a baking tray and set them inside the oven.
8. Bake for about 25 minutes until golden brown and let them cool off for another 15 minutes once done.
9. Serve warm.

Low-Carb Breakfast Sausage

Serves: 4

Ingredients

- 1 large green bell pepper
- 1 large red bell pepper
- 1 tsp. olive oil
- 1 tsp. spike seasoning
- ¼ tsp. ground black pepper
- About 12 sausages
- 55 grams low-fat mozzarella cheese, grated

Method

1. Preheat the oven to 215 C.
2. Grease a baking dish with some cooking spray.
3. Wash the bell peppers under some running water and pat them dry. Using a kitchen knife, dice them.
4. Place the bell peppers at the bottom of the baking dish. Drizzle some olive oil, sprinkle some seasoning, ground black pepper and place the tray inside the oven.
5. Bake the dish for about 20 minutes.
6. In the meanwhile, heat a saucepan over medium flame and add the sausages to it. Brown them from all sides for about 10-12 minutes all the while turning and tossing them.
7. Transfer the sausages on to a cutting board and slice them up into small pieces.
8. Once the peppers are baked, add the sausage slices along with some grated cheese on top. Bake for another 5 minutes.
9. Serve hot.

Spinach, Goat Cheese and Chorizo Omelet

Serves: 2

Ingredients

- 115 grams chorizo sausage
- 1 tsp. butter
- 4 large eggs
- 1 tbsp. water
- 140 grams goat cheese, crumbled or grated
- 360 grams baby spinach, thawed
- 45 grams sliced avocado
- 45 grams salsa Verde
- 1/8 tsp. salt
- ¼ tsp. ground black pepper

Method

1. Remove the sausage from the refrigerator and bring it to room temperature.
2. Heat a saucepan over medium flame and ass the sausages to it. Brown them for 12 minutes from all sides until fully cooked. Transfer them on paper towels.
3. In the meanwhile, crack the eggs in a large bowl. Add some water and beat them until smooth.
4. Melt some butter in the pan over low heat. Add the egg mixture to the pan, followed by some spinach and crumbled goat cheese on top. Sprinkle some salt and ground pepper and cover the pan with a lid.
5. Let it cook for 3 minutes on one side and then flip it over. Cook for another 2 minutes until the Centre seems fully cooked.
6. Transfer the omelet on a large plate.
7. Serve along with some sliced avocado and salsa verde.

Smoked Salmon and Egg Stuffed Avocados

Serves: 4

Ingredients

- 4 avocados
- 115 grams Smoked Salmon
- 8 medium eggs
- ¼ tsp. sea salt
- ½ tsp. ground black pepper
- ½ tsp. chili flakes
- 1 tsp. fresh dill

Method

1. Preheat the oven to 215 C.
2. Grease a baking tray with some cooking oil or butter.
3. Wash the avocados properly and pat them dry. Using a sharp knife, slice them up into two halves. Scoop out the flesh.
4. In a bowl, combine the eggs with smoked salmon, salt, ground pepper and mix well.
5. Place the avocados on the baking tray. Fill each of the avocado halves with the egg mixture and top it up with some red chili flakes and dill.
6. Bake for about 20 minutes and serve warm.

Keto Special Morning Meatloaf

Serves: 4

Ingredients

- 1 tsp. ghee or butter
- 6 large eggs
- 450 grams Italian sausage
- ¼ yellow onion, finely chopped
- 55 grams cheddar cheese, grated
- 2 tbsp. scallion

Method

1. Preheat the oven to 175 C.
2. Grease a baking pan using some cooking spray and set aside.
3. Place the sausages on a cutting board and chop them up it thick slices using a sharp knife.
4. In a bowl, crack the eggs and beat them lightly using a fork. Now add the sausage pieces, onion, and some cream cheese and whisk thoroughly.
5. Pour this batter into the baking tray and set it in the oven.
6. Bake for 30 minutes uncovered until it is golden brown.
7. Remove the dish from the oven and let it cool off for 5 minutes.
8. Now take the remaining cream cheese and spread it across the meatloaf. Add some grated cheese on top along with the scallions.
9. Place the tray in the oven and bake again for 5 minutes. Now broil it for 2-3 minutes until the cheese starts turning golden and crisp.
10. Serve warm.

Cajun Cauliflower Hash

Serves: 2

Ingredients

- 2 tbsp. olive oil
- 1 small onion, diced into 4 pieces
- 2 tbsp. minced garlic
- 450 grams cauliflower florets
- 1 tbsp. Cajun seasoning
- 220 grams red pastrami, shaved
- 1 small green bell pepper, diced into 4 pieces

Method

1. Heat some olive oil or ghee in a saucepan over medium flame.
2. Add some minced garlic, chopped onions and sauté them for about 3-4 minutes until they turn golden brown.
3. Boil some water in a vessel and add the cauliflower florets in it. Remove from flame and cover with a lid for 5 minutes. Once done, drain the water and add some cold water to the vessel. Now drain off the cold water too and using your hands, squeeze out all the excess water from the cauliflower florets.
4. Add the florets to the saucepan and fry for 10 minutes until it starts to brown.
5. Add some Cajun seasoning and toss all the ingredients well.
6. Slide in the chopped peppers and pastrami and mix. Cook for 5 minutes and remove from flame.
7. Transfer the mixture into a large bowl.
8. Fry an egg over the saucepan and place it on top.
9. Sprinkle some more Cajun seasoning and serve.

Keto and Grain Free Onion and Chive Cauliflower Hash Browns

Serves: 2

Ingredients

- 1 large head of cauliflower, approximately 1 lb.
- 1 large egg
- ¼ tsp. salt
- ¼ tsp. ground black pepper
- 1 tbsp. finely chopped onion
- 1 tbsp. finely chopped red bell pepper
- 1 tbsp. finely chopped green bell pepper
- 2 tbsp. Cotswold cheese
- 1 tsp. olive oil

Method

1. Wash the cauliflower properly and pat it dry. Now rice it using a grater. Set aside.
2. In a bowl, crack the eggs and beat them lightly. To this, add the cauliflower rice, some peppers, onion, salt, ground black pepper, and whisk well until nice and smooth.
3. Heat a saucepan over medium flame. Add some olive oil and spread it across the pan.
4. Add half of the cauliflower mix and spread it across the pan using a spatula.
5. Now let the hash brown cook for about 4-5 minutes until it starts turning golden brown and then flip it over.
6. Add some more onions and Cotswold cheese on top of the hash brown.
7. Let the hash brown cook until the cheese has slightly melted. Repeat the process with the remaining batter.
8. Serve warm.

Chapter 7: Keto Smoothies

Low Carb Smoothie

Serves: 6

Ingredients

- 950 ml water
- 180 grams romaine lettuce
- 60 grams pineapple, chopped
- 2 tbsp. fresh parsley
- 1 tbsp. minced ginger
- 180 grams cucumber, peeled and finely chopped
- ½ cup kiwi fruit, peeled and sliced
- ½ avocado, sliced
- 1 tbsp. sugar substitute
- Some ice cubes for serving

Method

1. Wash the lettuce leaves properly under some running water and roughly chop them using a kitchen knife.
2. Add them in a blender. To this, add chopped pineapple, ginger, cucumber, kiwi, avocado, sugar substitute and water.
3. Give all the ingredients a whisk. Now add some parsley and blend the mixture into a smooth paste. Make sure there are no lumps. You can also strain this juice if you wish.
4. Pour the smoothie into a large glass.
5. Add some ice cubes and serve chilled.

Chocolate Bing Smoothie Recipe

Serves: 2

Ingredients

- 1 large cup coconut milk, full fat
- ½ avocado, ripe
- 30 grams cacao powder
- 180 grams frozen cherries
- ¼ tsp. turmeric powder
- 230 ml cup water
- Some ice cubes for serving

Method

1. Wash the avocado properly under some running water and roughly chop it using a kitchen knife.
2. Add it to a blender. To this, add some cacao powder, roughly chopped cherries and turmeric powder and give it a whisk.
3. Add some water, coconut milk and blend all the ingredients until it forms a smooth paste. Ensure that the smoothie is completely lump free.
4. Pour it into a large glass and add some ice cubes to serve.
5. You can also refrigerate the smoothie for about 30 minutes before serving.

Coconut Milk Strawberry Smoothie

Serves: 2

Ingredients

- 180 grams frozen strawberries
- 230 ml coconut milk, unsweetened
- 2 tbsp. almond butter
- 1 tbsp. peanut butter
- 2 packets stevia
- 1 tsp. chia seeds
- Some crushed ice
- Some mint leaves

Method

1. Start by washing the strawberries properly under running water. Take their leave off and roughly chop them up using a sharp knife. Add them to a blender.
2. To this, add some almond butter, coconut milk, peanut butter, chia seeds, stevia drops and blend it using a hand blender. You can also add these ingredients to a food processor and whisk them until smooth. Make sure there are no lump formations.
3. Pour in a tall glass and add some crushed ice.
4. Garnish with mint leaves and serve.

Keto Sleep-In Smoothie

Serves: 2

Ingredients

- 1 large egg
- 60 ml Kombucha or coconut milk
- 180 grams of fruit (berries or musk melon)
- 365 grams baby spinach, thawed
- ¼ avocado, sliced
- Some crushed ice

Method

1. Wash the berries thoroughly under some running water and roughly chop them up using a sharp knife.
2. Similarly, wash the baby spinach and chop it up with the same knife.
3. Add the chopped spinach, berries and chopped avocado to the blender and whisk. Add some Kombucha, crack an egg and whisk again until smooth. Ensure that the mixture is completely lump-free.
4. Add some crushed ice to this smoothie and serve chilled.

Keto Tropical Smoothie

Serves: 2

Ingredients

- 175 ml cup coconut milk
- 60 ml sour cream
- 2 tbsp. flaxseed meal
- 1 tbsp. macadamia nut oil
- 20 drops of stevia
- ½ tsp. mango essence
- ¼ tsp. banana essence
- Some crushed ice

Method

1. Add the flax seed meal to some coconut milk in a bowl and let it soak up for 10 minutes.
2. To this, add some sour cream, macadamia oil, stevia, mango essence, banana essence and mix. Add this to a blender and whisk until smooth. Make sure to keep the smoothie lump free.
3. Pour into tall glasses and add some crushed ice to them.
4. Serve chilled.

Fat Burning Vanilla Smoothie

Serves: 1

Ingredients

- 2 large egg yolks
- 50 grams mascarpone cheese
- 60 ml water
- 1 tbsp. coconut oil
- ½ tsp. vanilla extract
- 3 drops of stevia
- Some crushed ice
- 2 tbsp. whipped cream

Method

1. Add the mascarpone cheese to a bowl and soften it using a spoon.
2. Add the cheese to a blender along with some water, coconut oil, vanilla extract, stevia, whipping cream and whisk until the mixture is nice and smooth. Ensure there are no lumps.
3. Pour into a tall glass and add some crushed ice.
4. Serve chilled.

Avocado Smoothie

Serves: 2

Ingredients

- 240 ml almond milk
- 90 grams whipping cream
- 1 medium avocado
- 6 drops of stevia
- ½ tsp. vanilla essence
- Some crushed ice cubes

Method

1. Wash the avocado properly and pat it dry. Peel the skin off using a peeler and slice it up using a knife.
2. Add the avocado to a blender along with whipping cream, almond milk, stevia, and vanilla essence and blend it for about 2 minutes on high until the mixture turns out to be smooth and frothy.
3. Pour into a tall glass and add some crushed ice.
4. Serve chilled.

Blueberry Galaxy

Serves: 1

Ingredients

- 240 ml coconut milk
- 90 grams blueberries
- 1 tsp. vanilla essence
- Half ripe banana
- 1 tsp. coconut oil
- 1 scoop whey protein powder (optional)
- Some crushed ice

Method

1. Wash the berries thoroughly under some running water and roughly chop them up using a sharp knife. Using the same knife, slice up the banana.
2. Add the berries and banana slices to a blender, followed by vanilla essence, coconut oil, whey protein powder, coconut milk and whisk using a hand blender or use a food processor. Blend until the mixture turns out to be smooth and lump-free.
3. Pour into a tall glass and add some crushed ice.
4. Serve chilled.

Keto Pumpkin Smoothie

Serves: 2

Ingredients

- 60 ml pumpkin puree, homemade or canned
- 60 ml almond milk
- 1 scoop whey protein powder (optional)
- 60 ml coconut milk
- ½ tsp. pumpkin pie spice powder
- 3 drops of stevia
- 1 tbsp. extra virgin coconut oil
- 25 grams whipped cream
- Some crushed ice

Method

1. Combine all the ingredients except crushed ice and add them to a blender. Blend for 2 to 3 minutes on high until you get a smooth, lump-free mixture.
2. Pour into a tall glass and add some crushed ice.
3. Serve chilled.

Ketogenic Peanut Butter Milkshake

Serves: 1

Ingredients

- ½ cup coconut cream
- 1 cup almond or coconut milk
- 1 tsp. vanilla essence
- 2 tbsp. peanut butter
- 2 drops of stevia
- Some crushed ice
- Some chopped almonds

Method

1. Add all the ingredients to a blender except crushed ice and almonds. Blend it on high for about one minute until the mixture is nice and frothy. Ensure that the mixture is lump free.
2. Pour into a tall glass and add some chopped almonds on top.
3. Add come-crushed ice and serve.

Chapter 8: Fish

Herby Keto Style Baked Fish

Serves: 4

Ingredients

- 4 large fish fillets
- ½ tsp. rosemary
- 1 tsp. thyme
- 1 tsp. dried basil
- ½ tsp. salt
- 1/8 tsp. ground black pepper
- 1 tsp. paprika
- 1 tbsp. olive oil
- Some cherry tomatoes garnish

Method

1. Preheat the oven to 176 C.
2. Grease a baking dish with some oil.
3. Clean the fish fillets properly and lay them on a large plate. Now coat the fish with olive oil from all sides.
4. In a small bowl, combine paprika with rosemary, thyme, basil, salt, pepper and mix well.
5. Rub this spice mixture all over the fish. Make sure that the fish is completely dipped in the spice mix.
6. Transfer the fish on a baking dish and bake them for about 25 minutes until nice and crisp.
7. Transfer on a plate and serve along with some cherry tomatoes on the side.

Parmesan Tilapia

Serves: 4

Ingredients

- 4 medium tilapia fillets
- 50 grams parmesan cheese, grated
- 60 ml butter
- 4 tbsp. mayonnaise
- 2 tbsp. lemon juice
- ½ tsp. garlic powder
- ½ tsp. dried basil
- ½ tsp. ground black pepper
- 1/4 tsp. sea salt
- ¼ tsp. onion powder

Method

1. Clean the tilapia fillet properly and pat them dry using paper towels.
2. Melt some butter in a saucepan over medium heat and drizzle it over the fillets.
3. In a small bowl, combine dried basil, salt, pepper, garlic powder, onion powder, lemon juice and mix well with a spoon.
4. Coat the fish generously with the above mixture and set them in the refrigerator for 45 minutes.
5. Combine the grated cheese and mayonnaise in a bowl and whisk it until it softens. You can also use an electric beater to make a smooth paste.
6. Remove the fish from the refrigerator and dip them in the cheese mixture. Make sure that the fish is completely coated with this mixture.
7. Switch the broiler on and let it heat up. Set the fish in a foil and gently place them on the broiler.
8. Broil for 2-3 minutes on each side until the fish is properly cooked.
9. Serve hot.

Squid Noodle Pasta

Serves: 2

Ingredients:

- 290 grams squid tubes (calamari), rinsed, cleaned
- 60 ml chicken stock
- 90 grams mushrooms, sliced
- 240 ml low carb tomato sauce
- 1 clove garlic, sliced
- 2 tbsp. yellow onion, chopped
- 60 ml white wine
- 2 tbsp. olive oil
- 50 grams Parmesan cheese, grated
- Salt to taste
- Pepper powder to taste
- 2 tbsp. fresh basil, chopped
- A pinch stevia (optional)

Instructions:

1. Place the squid tubes on your cutting board. Slit open one side of the tube so as to lay the tube flat. Now cut the tube lengthwise so that you get long strips of squid, which is now your pasta.
2. Place a skillet over medium heat. Add onions and garlic and sauté until translucent.
3. Add wine and mix. Add tomato sauce and mix. Add stock and let it simmer for a couple of minutes.
4. Add stevia if desired and mix.
5. Add mushroom, squid pasta, salt and pepper and stir.
6. Cover and cook until pasta is tender.
7. Add basil and stir. Remove from heat.
8. Serve garnished with cheese.

Pan Seared Trout with Orange, Butter and Pecan Sauce

Serves: 2

Ingredients

- 1 large fillet
- 1 tbsp. olive oil
- ½ tsp. sea salt
- ½ tsp. ground black pepper
- 1 tbsp. butter
- 1 medium orange
- ½ cup chopped pecans
- Some freshly chopped parsley for garnish

Method

1. Wash the orange and pat it dry. Now with the help of a grater, gently zest it.
2. Clean the fish fillets properly and pat them dry using paper towels. Season them generously with the orange zest, some salt and pepper and set them aside for about 30 minutes. You can also rest them in the refrigerator for 30 minutes but ensure that you allow the fish to come to room temperature before you start cooking.
3. In a saucepan, heat some olive oil on medium flame. Spread the oil across the pan by twisting and turning it.
4. Place the fish on the pan. Sear the fillet for about 3-4 minutes from each side until it starts turning crisp. Once done, remove on a large plate.
5. Place the pecans on a cutting board and roughly chop them using a sharp knife.
6. Now melt some butter in the same pan and add the chopped pecans. Fry them for about one minute and remove from heat.
7. Drizzle the pecans on top of the fish.
8. Garnish with some chopped parsley and serve immediately.

Lake Trout with Butter Sauce

Serves: 4

Ingredients

- 4 large fresh trout or fish of your choice
- 2 tbsp. olive oil
- 4 tbsp. of butter
- ½ tsp. sea salt
- ½ tsp. ground black pepper
- 3 tbsp. chopped chives
- 3 tsp. lemon zest
- 2 tsp. freshly squeezed lemon juice

Method

1. Clean the trout and drizzle it with some olive oil.
2. Brush the grill with some oil and let it heat up. Place the fish on top and grill them for about 4 minutes on each side.
3. In the meanwhile, melt some butter in a saucepan over medium flame. To this, add some chopped chives, lemon zest and lemon juice.
4. Let it cook for 2-3 minutes on low flame. Make sure that you don't boil the mixture, just let it melt. Sprinkle some salt and pepper and mix well.
5. Transfer the grilled fish in the pan and cook for another 30 seconds from each side until it soaks up the entire liquid.
6. Transfer on a large plate and serve immediately.

Keto Fish Fritters

Serves: 4

Ingredients

- 4 large sardines
- 60 grams psyllium
- 4 large eggs
- 360 grams fresh cilantro
- ½ tsp. salt
- ½ tsp. ground black pepper
- 60 grams coconut flour
- 4 tbsp. coconut oil, for frying

Method

1. Clean the sardines properly and add them to a large bowl. Now using a spatula, mash the sardines well by breaking them into small pieces.
2. To this, add some salt, ground pepper, and psyllium and mix well.
3. In another bowl, crack the eggs and whisk them properly using a fork. Pour this mixture into the above bowl and mix again.
4. In the meanwhile, wash the cilantro properly and chop it finely using a sharp kitchen knife. I prefer leaving it slightly coarse.
5. Add the chopped cilantro to the bowl and mix to form slightly firm dough. Now using your hands start forming small patties out of it and keep them aside.
6. Spread the coconut flour on a flat dish.
7. Add about 1 tbsp. coconut oil to the skillet and let it heat up. Dip 3 patties in the coconut flour mixture form both sides and place them on the skillet.
8. Fry them for about 3 to 4 minutes on each side until golden brown. Repeat this process for the remaining patties while ensuring that you wipe the skillet with a paper towel after each batch. This will prevent the flour from burning.
9. Serve the patties warm.

Salmon Meatballs with Garlic Lemon Cream Sauce

Serves: 6

Ingredients

- 2 tbsp. butter
- 60 grams cup onion, finely chopped
- 2 minced garlic cloves
- 500 grams wild caught salmon
- 2 tbsp. Dijon mustard
- 45 grams chopped chives
- 1 large egg
- 1 tbsp. coconut flour
- 1 tsp. salt

For the lemon cream sauce

- 2 tbsp. butter
- 4 minced garlic cloves
- Zest of one lemon
- 1 tbsp. lemon juice
- 2 tbsp. Dijon mustard
- 480 ml cream
- 2 tbsp. chopped chives

Method

1. Preheat the oven to 177 C.
2. Melt some butter in a skillet over medium heat. Add some minced garlic, chopped onions and sauté until they turn golden brown. Set it aside.
3. In a large bowl, add the salmon and mash it up using a fork or a spatula. To this, add some Dijon mustard, chives, egg, coconut flour, salt and mix well. Using your hands, make a roll out a few meatballs.
4. Place them on a greased baking tray and bake for about 20-25 minutes until the sides turn golden brown.
5. In the meanwhile, start making the cream sauce. Melt some butter on a large skillet over medium heat. Sauté some minced garlic for about 2 to 3 minutes.
6. Add some lemon juice, Dijon mustard, chives and mix. Add some fresh cream and simmer for about 5 to 7 minutes while whisking it.
7. Remove the meatballs from the oven and add them to the pan. Cook for another minute and remove from flame.
8. Serve them hot.

Grilled Salmon with Avocado Salsa

Serves: 4

Ingredients

- 900 grams Salmon, sliced into 4 pieces
- 1 tbsp. olive oil
- 1 tsp. salt
- 1 tsp. ground cumin
- 1 tsp. paprika
- 1 tsp. onion powder
- 1/21 tsp. ancho chili powder
- 1 tsp. ground black pepper
- For the avocado salsa
- 1 medium avocado
- ½ red onion, thinly sliced
- 2 tbsp. chopped cilantro
- 1/8 tsp. salt

Method

1. Clean the salmon properly and pat it dry. Now coat the fish with olive oil from all sides.
2. In a bowl, combine paprika, ground cumin, ancho chili, black pepper, salt, and onion powder and mix well.
3. Dip the fish in this spice mixture and rub it all over. Ensure that the spice mix is generously spread across all sides of the fish. Refrigerate the fish for about 30 minutes.
4. Bring the fish to room temperature before you start cooking it.
5. Preheat the grill.
6. Place the fish on top and grill it for 5 minutes on each side until it turns crisp.
7. In the meanwhile, wash the avocado properly under running water and pat it dry using a paper towel. Using a sharp knife cut it into thin slices.
8. Add the avocado slice to a large bowl along with onion, cilantro, salt, lime juice and mix well. You can also let this mixture chill in the refrigerator for 15 to 20 minutes until you are ready to use it.
9. Place the grilled salmon on a large plate.
10. Add the avocado mixture on top and serve.

Salmon Avocado and Salsa

Serves: 4 or 5

Ingredients

- 900 grams salmon
- 2 large avocados
- 2 tbsp. cilantro, chopped
- 3 tbsp. lemon juice
- 1 tbsp. onion powder
- 1 small red onion, finely chopped
- 3 bell peppers (assorted), chopped
- 1 tsp. smoked paprika
- 1 tsp. salt, divided
- 1 tsp. ground black pepper
- 1 tbsp. olive oil
- 1 tsp. cumin powder

Method

1. Preheat the oven to 188 C.
2. Grease a baking pan with some cooking spray and set aside.
3. Wash the avocadoes under some running water and pat them dry. Cut them into small pieces using a sharp knife. Transfer them to a bowl.
4. To this, add chopped red onion, bell peppers, cilantro, onion powder, lemon juice, some salt and mix well using a spoon. Set it inside the fish for an hour.
5. Clean the Salmon properly and pat it dry using paper towels.
6. IN a small bowl, combine paprika, salt, black pepper, cumin powder and mix. Now rub some olive oil all over the salmon, followed by the spice mix. Make sure you coat the fish generously with the spice mixture.
7. Place the fish on the baking tray and set it inside the oven. Bake for 12-14 minutes until the sides turn crisp.
8. Serve the fish on a large plate along with some avocado salsa on the side.

Low Carb Fish Cakes

Serves: 2

Ingredients

- 360 grams cauliflower, coarsely grinder
- 360 grams white fish
- 1 tbsp. scallions
- 2 tsp. old bay seasoning
- ½ tsp. sea salt
- ½ tsp. ground black pepper
- 1 large egg
- 1 tbsp. scallions
- 110 grams flax crackers, grounded
- 2 tbsp. butter to fry the cakes

Method

1. Clean the fish properly and cook them in a steamer or a skillet until they turn slightly tender.
2. Add the fish to a large bowl. To this, add cauliflower puree, old bay seasoning, chopped cilantro, chopped scallions, eggs and mix well using a spoon. You can also mash the fish using a spatula and then add all the ingredients and mix well. Just ensure that you don't over pulverize the fish. Set this mixture in the refrigerator for about 30 minutes.
3. Remove from fridge and using your hands, make circular patties out of the dough.
4. Spread the crushed crackers on a plate. Dip the patties in this mixture form both sides and set them aside.
5. Melt some butter on a large skillet over medium flame. Once the skillet heats up, place the cakes on it and fry them for about 4 minutes on each side until they turn brown and crisp. You can also drizzle some olive oil on top.
6. Serve on a large plate along with some chopped cilantro.

Low Carb Fish Tacos

Serves: 4

Ingredients

- 2 tbsp. olive oil
- ½ small yellow onion, sliced
- 1 medium jalapeno, chopped
- 2 minced garlic cloves
- 2 tbsp. butter
- 120 ml chipotle pepper in adobo sauce
- 2 tbsp. butter
- 450 grams haddock fillets
- 4 wholegrain tortillas
- ½ tsp. salt
- ¼ tsp. ground black pepper
- ¼ tsp. paprika
- Some chopped coriander for garnish

Method

1. Clean the fish fillets but gently removing the bones.
2. In a small bowl, combine some salt, pepper, paprika and mix well using a spoon.
3. Coat the fish generously with this mixture by rubbing it all over. Now refrigerate the fish for about 20 minutes. Don't forget to bring the fish to room temperature before you start cooking them.
4. Add some olive oil to a saucepan and heat it on medium flame.
5. Add minced garlic and chopped onion to the pan and sauté it for about 2 to 3 minutes until they turn golden brown. Keep stirring while you fry them.
6. Transfer the chipotle peppers to a cutting board and chop them up into slices using a sharp knife. Add them to the pan along with the adobo sauce and mix well using a large wooden spoon.
7. Now add some butter, mayonnaise and stir.
8. Finally, place the fish fillets on the pan and cook them for about 2 minutes on high flame from each side. You don't want to burn the fish but ensure they turn super crispy. Once done, remove from flame and allow it to cool down.
9. Fill a bit of this mixture into each of the tortillas and add some chopped coriander on top and serve.

Keto Style Spicy Fish Stew

Serves: 4

Ingredients

- 450 grams wild caught fish
- 1 tbsp. lemon juice
- 1 medium jalapeno pepper, sliced
- 1 medium onion, finely chopped
- 1 medium onion yellow bell pepper, sliced
- 1 medium onion red bell pepper, sliced
- 1 medium onion green bell pepper, sliced
- 2 minced garlic cloves
- 1 tsp. paprika
- 480 ml chicken broth
- 480 ml chopped tomatoes
- 1 tsp. sea salt
- 1/2 tsp. ground black pepper
- 450 ml coconut milk
- Some chopped cilantro and lemon wedges for garnishing

Method

1. Clean the fish, drizzle some lemon juice on them and refrigerate for 20 minutes. Bring the fish to room temperature before you proceed with the cooking.
2. Add some olive oil to a saucepan and heat it on medium flame.
3. Add minced garlic and chopped onion to the pan and sauté it for about 2 to 3 minutes until they turn golden brown. Keep stirring while you fry them.
4. Add chopped bell peppers and fry for another 2 minutes until slightly tender.
5. Slide in the tomatoes, spices and cook or 2 to 3 minutes.
6. Now pour the chicken broth into the pan and stir all the ingredients well using a large wooden spoon.
7. To this, add some salt, pepper and simmer for 15 minutes.
8. Pour some coconut milk along with the fish and stir again. Allow the liquid to come to a boil and then reduce the flame.
9. Cover the pan and cook on low heat for about 10-12 minutes.
10. Transfer the stew in a large bowl and garnish with some chopped cilantro and lemon wedges.
11. Serve hot.

Keto Style Sri Lankan Fish Curry

Serves: 5

Ingredients

- 115 grams white fish
- 4 tbsp. coconut oil
- 1/2 tsp. mustard seeds
- 2 medium green chilies, slit
- 1 tsp. freshly grated ginger
- ¼ tsp. ground cumin
- 1 tsp. curry powder
- ½ tsp. turmeric powder
- ½ red onion, finely chopped
- 3 minced garlic cloves
- 360 ml coconut cream, full fat
- ½ tsp. sea salt
- ¼ tsp. ground black pepper
- 120 ml water
- Chopped coriander or parsley for garnish

Method

1. Clean the fish properly and season it with some salt and pepper and set it aside for about 20 minutes. You can also refrigerate them for 20 minutes but remember to bring them to room temperature before you start cooking.
2. Heat some coconut oil in a large saucepan over medium flame.
3. Add mustard seeds and let them pop.
4. Add minced garlic and chopped onion to the pan and sauté it for about 2 to 3 minutes until they turn golden brown. Keep stirring while you fry them.
5. Add some cumin, turmeric powder, slit green chilies, curry powder and cook for another 30 seconds.
6. Pour some coconut milk into the pan and mix all the ingredients well using a large wooden spoon. Let the mixture simmer for about 20 minutes on low heat.
7. In the meanwhile, heat another saucepan over medium flame and place the fish on it. Let them cook for 2 to 3 minutes on each side until nice and brown.
8. Add the fish to the curry and cook all the ingredients for about 5 minutes on medium flame. Ensure that you don't overcook the fish.
9. Once done, quickly remove from flame and transfer to a large bowl.
10. Garnish with some chopped cilantro and serve hot.

Chapter 9: Poultry

Pesto Chicken Casserole with Feta Cheese and Olives

Serves: 4

Ingredients

- 680 grams chicken breasts or thighs
- 100 grams red pesto
- 100 grams whipping cream
- 8 tbsp. olives, pitted
- 225 grams feta cheese, crumbled
- 1 tsp. minced garlic
- 1 tsp. salt
- ½ tsp. ground black pepper
- ½ tsp. smoked paprika
- 4 tbsp. butter for frying
- Some leafy green for serving
- Some cherry tomatoes
- 1 tbsp. extra virgin olive oil

Method

1. Preheat the oven to 188 C.
2. Grease a baking pan with some oil or butter and set aside.
3. Clean the chicken thighs properly and pat them dry using paper towels. Now transfer them on a cutting board and cut them into large pieces using a sharp knife. Season them generously with some salt and pepper and place them in the refrigerator for 15 to 20 minutes. Remove them and allow them to come to room temperature.
4. Melt some butter over medium flame and spread it across the pan. Place the chicken thighs on the pan and fry them for 4 minutes on each side until they turn golden brown.
5. Once done, add the chicken thighs to a large bowl. To this, add some pesto, olives, whipping cream, crumbled feta cheese, minced garlic and mix well.
6. Add the mixture to a baking dish and bake for 25-30 minutes until you start seeing bubbles forming around the chicken and it turns light brown.
7. Place some leafy greens on a large dish. Gently place the chicken on top. Add some cherry tomatoes, drizzle some extra virgin olive oil on top and serve.

Creamy Chicken Casserole

Serves: 4

Ingredients

- 900 grams chicken thighs
- 200 grams parmesan cheese, shredded
- 100 grams sour cream or whipping cream
- 110 grams cauliflower florets
- 1 medium leek, chopped
- 115 grams fresh cherry tomatoes
- 2 tbsp. green pesto
- 1 tbsp. lemon juice
- 3 tbsp. butter
- ½ tsp. salt
- ½ tsp. ground black pepper

Method

1. Preheat the oven to 188 C.
2. Grease a baking pan with some oil or butter and set aside.
3. Clean the chicken thighs properly and pat them dry using paper towels. Now transfer them on a cutting board and cut them into large pieces using a sharp knife. Season them generously with some salt and pepper and place them in the refrigerator for 15 to 20 minutes. Remove them and allow them to come to room temperature.
4. Melt some butter over medium flame and spread it across the pan. Place the chicken thighs on the pan and fry them for 4 minutes on each side until they turn golden brown.
5. In a bowl, combine sour cream with pesto, lemon juice and mix well with a spoon.
6. Place the browned chicken thighs on the baking dish and pour the sour cream mixture on top.
7. Top the chicken with some cherry tomatoes, chopped leek and cauliflower florets.
8. Sprinkle some cheese on top of the chicken and bake it for about 30 minutes or slightly more until it turns completely brown. Ensure that you don't burn the chicken.
9. Serve immediately.

Chicken Breasts with Herby Butter

Serves: 4

Ingredients

- 4 large chicken breasts
- 30 ml butter or olive oil
- ¾ tsp. sea salt
- ¾ tsp. ground black pepper

For the herby butter

- 150 grams butter
- 1 minced garlic clove
- ½ tsp. garlic powder
- ¼ tsp. salt
- 1 tsp. lemon juice
- 1/8 tsp. ground black pepper
- ½ tsp. rosemary
- ½ tsp. thyme
- ½ tsp. oregano
- Some leafy greens for serving

Method

1. Preheat the oven to 177 C.
2. Grease a baking pan with some oil or butter and set aside.
3. Clean the chicken breasts properly and pat them dry using paper towels. Now transfer them on a cutting board and cut them into large pieces using a sharp knife. Season them generously with some salt and pepper and place them in the refrigerator for 15 to 20 minutes. Remove them and allow them to come to room temperature.
4. Start with making the herb butter. Melt some butter in a saucepan over medium heat. Once done, add it to a bowl. To this, add some minced garlic, garlic powder, rosemary, oregano, thyme, salt, pepper, lemon juice and mix well. Let the butter sit at room temperature until it's time to serve.
5. Place the chicken on a greased baking dish and bake for about 20 minutes. Now flip the chicken and bake for another 15 minutes until it is nice and brown.
6. Place some leafy greens on a large dish and place the chicken on top.
7. Drizzle some herb butter on top and serve hot.

Keto Chicken Salad

Serves: 6

Ingredients:

- 6 chicken tenders
- 1 onion, chopped
- 6 radish, halved
- 1 tbsp. fresh dill, chopped
- 1 stalk celery, chopped
- 50 grams mayonnaise
- 1 tsp. salt
- 1 tsp. pepper powder
- 45 grams minced dill pickle
- Cooking spray

Instructions:

1. Place the chicken in a greased baking dish and bake at 218° C until it is done.
2. Place radish in another baking dish and spray with cooking spray. Place in the oven and bake until it is done.
3. Remove from oven and cool. Chop radish into smaller pieces and place in a serving dish.
4. Add chicken and rest of the ingredients to it and toss well.
5. Chill for a while and serve.

Low Carb Chicken Alfredo

Serves: 4

Ingredients

- 4 large eggs
- 6 egg yolks
- 180 ml water
- 2 tbsp. olive oil
- 6 tbsp. psyllium husk powder
- 4 tbsp. coconut flour
- 2 tsp. herbal salt

For the sauce

- 900 grams chicken breasts
- 150 grams fried bacon
- 100 grams whipping cream or sour cream
- 180 ml milk
- 75 grams parmesan cheese, grated
- 4 minced garlic cloves
- 4 tbsp. green pesto
- 1 tsp. salt
- ½ tsp. ground black pepper
- 8 large button mushrooms
- 1 large red bell pepper, sliced
- 4 tbsp. butter for frying

Method

1. Preheat the oven to 177 C.
2. Grease a baking pan with some oil or butter and set aside.
3. In a large bowl, crack the eggs; add the egg yolk, olive oil and whish until they are nice and fluffy. You can also use an electric beater to whisk them. Just ensure that you don't overdo it.
4. To this, add some coconut powder, Phyllis husk powder, some salt and whish again.
5. Now spread the batter on two separate sheets of parchment paper. Place a thin plastic foil on top of it and roll it out. Try spreading the batter evenly. Now remove the plastic and place the parchment sheets on the baking tray. Bake them for 10 minutes and remove the parchment paper. Cut it into thin strips.

6. Clean the chicken breasts properly and pat them dry using paper towels. Now transfer them on a cutting board and cut them into large pieces using a sharp knife. Season them generously with some salt and pepper and place them in the refrigerator for 15 to 20 minutes. Remove them and allow them to come to room temperature.

7. Melt some butter in a saucepan and add the chicken pieces to it. Fry them along with the chopped peppers until golden. Now place the chicken pieces on a baking dish along with some bacon, Parmesan cheese and bake for 10 minutes. Transfer on a large plate.

8. Add a tsp. of olive oil to another saucepan and allow it to heat up. Add minced garlic and sauté them until golden. Add mushrooms, pesto and cook for 3 to 4 minutes. Add some milk, whipping cream and bring the mixture to a boil.

9. Place the egg strips on top of the chicken and bacon mixture. Pour the sauce on top and serve.

Buffalo Drumsticks with Chili Aioli

Serves: 4

Ingredients

- 900 grams chicken drumsticks or wings
- 2 tbsp. coconut oil or olive oil
- 2 tbsp. white wine vinegar
- 1 tbsp. thick tomato paste
- 1 tsp. salt
- 1 tsp. paprika powder
- 1 tbsp. tobasco sauce

Chili aioli

- 65 grams mayonnaise
- 1 tbsp. smoked paprika
- 1 tsp. minced garlic

Method

1. Preheat the oven to 215 C.
2. Grease a baking pan with some oil or butter and set aside.
3. In a bowl, combine white wine vinegar with some salt, paprika powder, tomato paste, tobacco sauce, coconut oil and mix well using a spoon.
4. Clean the chicken drumsticks properly and pat them dry using paper towels. Season them generously with some salt and pepper. Now coat them with the marinade and place them in the refrigerator for 15 to 20 minutes. You can also add the marinade to a zip lock bag along with the chicken and shake well before refrigerating. Remove them and allow them to come to room temperature.
5. Place the chicken drumsticks on the baking dish and bake for about 35 to 40 minutes until properly browned. You can cook them for 5 more minutes to brown them slightly more. Once done, transfer the chicken on a large dish.
6. In a large bowl, combine mayonnaise, paprika, minced garlic and mix well.
7. Add the aioli sauce on top and serve.

Chicken Skewers with Celery Fries and Spinach Dip

Serves: 4

Ingredients

Chicken skewers

- 8 wooden skewers
- 4 large chicken breasts
- 1 tsp. sea salt
- ½ tsp. ground black pepper
- 2 tbsp. olive oil

For the spinach dip

- 2 tbsp. olive oil
- 30 grams baby spinach, chopped
- 2 tbsp. dried parsley
- 1 tbsp. dried dill
- 1 tsp. onion powder
- ½ tsp. sea salt
- ¼ tsp. ground black pepper
- 100 grams mayonnaise
- 4 tbsp. sour cream
- 1 tbsp. lemon juice

Celery fries

- 450 grams root celery
- 2 tbsp. olive oil
- ½ tsp. sea salt
- ¼ tsp. ground black pepper

Method

1. Preheat the oven to 188 C.
2. Grease a baking pan with some oil or butter and set aside.
3. Start making the dip by adding all the ingredients to a large bowl. If you want, you finely chop the spinach for the dip. Mix all the ingredients with a spoon and let it sit in the fridge for about 20 minutes.
4. Clean the chicken breasts properly and pat them dry using paper towels. Now transfer them on a cutting board and cut them into large pieces using a sharp knife.

65

Season them generously with some salt, olive oil and pepper and place them in the refrigerator for 15 to 20 minutes. Remove them and allow them to come to room temperature.

5. Now insert the chicken pieces in the skewers, 5 or 6 at a time.
6. Broil the skewers for about 20 to 22 minutes until the chicken is completely cooked.
7. Peel and slice the celery root into strips using a sharp knife. Add some salt and pepper to them and mix well.
8. Spread out the roots on a baking tray and bake for 20 until nice and crispy.
9. Transfer the chicken skewers to a large plate and serve along with the celery fries and the spinach dip.

Chicken Liver with Thyme and Butter

Serve: 4

Ingredients

- For the Chicken liver
- 1 red onion
- 1 tsp. minced garlic clove
- 4 tbsp. butter
- 2 tbsp. port wine or brandy or whichever liquor you prefer
- 1 tbsp. thick tomato paste
- 450 grams chicken liver
- ¾ tsp. salt
- ¼ tsp. ground black pepper

Thyme butter

- 110 grams butter
- 1 tbsp. dried thyme
- 1 tsp. ground black pepper
- Some chopped dill for garnish

Method

1. Peel the red onion and chop it finely using a sharp kitchen knife.
2. Clean the chicken livers properly and pat them dry using paper towels. Now transfer them on a cutting board and cut them into large pieces using a sharp knife. Season them generously with some salt, olive oil and pepper and place them in the refrigerator for 15 to 20 minutes. Remove them and allow them to come to room temperature.
3. Melt some butter on a saucepan over medium heat. Add minced garlic, chopped onion and sauté until it turns golden brown. Keep stirring to make sure that you don't burn them.
4. Now add some tomato paste and cook for a minute. Allow it to cool down and add this mixture to a blender and blend it until smooth. Add this mixture back to the pan.
5. Add the chicken liver to the pan and cook for 5 to 6 minutes until it turns brown.
6. To this, add some port wine and cook for another couple of minutes until it starts releasing flavor.
7. IN the meanwhile, melt some butter in another saucepan. Add some thyme, black pepper and cook for about 30 seconds.
8. Transfer the chicken livers to a large plate. Pour the thyme butter on top.
9. Garnish with some chopped dill and serve.

Low-Carb Chicken Curry Pie

Serves: ingredients

For the pie crust

- 90 grams almond flour
- 4 tbsp. sesame seeds
- 4 tbsp. coconut flour
- 1 tbsp. psyllium powder
- 1 tsp. baking powder
- 1/4 tsp. salt
- 3 tbsp. olive oil or coconut oil
- 1 large egg
- 4 tbsp. water

For the filling

- 300 grams chicken thighs
- 100 grams mayonnaise
- 3 large eggs
- ½ green bell pepper, sliced
- 1 tsp. curry powder
- ½ tsp. paprika powder
- ½ tsp. sea salt
- ½ tsp. onion powder
- ¼ tsp. ground black pepper
- 8 tbsp. cream cheese
- 100 grams parmesan cheese, shredded

Method

1. Preheat the oven to 165 C.
2. Grease a baking dish with some oil or butter.
3. Clean the chicken thighs properly and pat them dry using paper towels. Now transfer them on a cutting board and cut them into large pieces using a sharp knife. Cook the chicken in a pan or broiler for about 10-12 minutes on high heat. Set aside.
4. Combine all the ingredients for the piecrust and put them in a food processor. Whisk for a few minutes until it forms a firm dough. If you do not own a food processor, you can simply mash the ingredients with a fork and form a dough using your hands. Keep this dough aside for about 20 minutes to firm up.

5. Place a parchment paper on the baking dish so the pie does not stick.
6. Spread the dough evenly across the baking dish using a spatula. Bake for about 15 minutes until the piecrust is crispy and brown.
7. Remove the crust and let it rest for 5 to 7 minutes.
8. IN the meanwhile, combine all the ingredients for the filling in a large bowl along with the sliced chicken and mix well.
9. Fill the piecrust with this mixture and bake for about 40 minutes until it golden brown.
10. Using a sharp knife to slice it up and serve warm.

Shredded Chicken Chili

Serves: 4

Ingredients

- 4 large chicken breasts or thighs
- 2 tbsp. butter
- 1 small onion, finely chopped
- 710 ml of chicken broth
- 360 grams diced ripe tomatoes
- 1 tbsp. red chili paste
- 1 tsp. smoked paprika
- 1 tbsp. cumin powder
- 1 tbsp. minced garlic
- 2 jalapeno chilies, chopped
- 180 ml cream cheese
- 1 tsp. salt
- ½ tsp. ground black pepper
- Some chopped coriander for garnish

Method

1. Clean the chicken thighs properly and pat them dry using paper towels.
2. Add some water to a large pot and bring it to a boil. Insert the chicken and cover the lid. Cook the chicken until it turns pink. Once done, drain out the excess water and place it on a cutting board. Shred it using two forks. You can also pressure cook the chicken breasts for 5 minutes and then give a natural release. Whatever works for you!
3. Melt some butter on a saucepan over medium heat.
4. Add chopped onions, minced garlic and cook until they turn completely golden brown. Keep stirring them all the while to keep them from burning.
5. To this, add shredded chicken, tomato paste, some diced tomatoes, chili paste, paprika, cumin powder and mix well using a large wooden spoon. Cook for 5 minutes and then add chopped jalapeno chili. Cook for another minute.
6. Pour some chicken broth into the pan and bring the mixture to a boil. Add some salt, pepper and let the mixture simmer for another 10 minutes.
7. Slice the cream cheese using a sharp knife and add it to the pot. Stir the mixture once again and cook for 5 minutes until the cream cheese get completely blended.
8. Transfer in a large bowl, garnish with some chopped coriander and serve hot.

Chicken Shawarma

Serves: 2

Ingredients

- 450 grams boneless chicken breasts

For the marinade

- 3 tbsp. butter
- 1 tbsp. ground cumin
- 1 tsp. sea salt
- 1 tsp. all spice powder
- 1 tsp. garlic powder
- ¼ tsp. cinnamon powder
- ½ tsp. ground black pepper
- ½ tsp. hot sauce
- ½ tsp. minced ginger
- ½ tsp. smoked paprika
- ¼ tsp. cardamom powder

For garnish

- 6 Kalamata olives
- 1 medium radish, peeled and sliced into thin strips
- 1 tsp. capers

Method

1. Preheat the oven to 188 C.
2. Grease a baking dish with some cooking spray.
3. Combine all the ingredients for the marinade in a bowl including olive oil, cumin, salt, pepper, paprika, all spice powder, garlic powder, cinnamon powder, cardamom powder, hot sauce, minced ginger and mix well.
4. Clean the chicken thighs properly and pat them dry using paper towels.
5. Season them generously with the spice mix by rubbing it all over the chicken and place them in the refrigerator for 4 minutes. Remove them and allow them to come to room temperature.
6. Place the chicken on the baking tray and drizzle some olive oil on top if you wish. Bake for about 20 minutes until nice and golden. Make sure that the chicken is properly cooked.
7. Transfer the chicken in a large plate.
8. Garnish with olives, radish strips, and capers and serve immediately.

Spinach Stuffed Chicken Breasts

Serves: 3

Ingredients

- 3 large chicken breasts
- 1450 grams baby spinach, thawed
- 85 grams feta cheese
- 115 grams cream cheese, softened
- 1 minced garlic clove
- ½ tsp. sea salt
- ¼ tsp. ground black pepper
- 1 tbsp. olive oil

Method

1. Preheat the oven to 216 C.
2. Grease the baking pan with cooking oil or butter.
3. Place the spinach on a cutting board and chop it roughly using a sharp kitchen knife. Add it to a large bowl.
4. Using your hands, crumble some feta cheese and add it to the same bowl. To this, add some garlic, cream cheese and mix well. You can keep this mixture in the fridge until you start filling the chicken.
5. Clean the chicken breasts properly and pat it dry using paper towels. Now hold a kitchen knife in one hand and place the other hand on top of the chicken breast. Slowly start making a slit from inside the chicken breast and slice it down until its thinnest part to make a pocket. You will have to be very careful while doing this otherwise you may hurt yourself.
6. Separate the spinach mixture into three equal parts and fill each of the chicken breasts with it. Season them with some salt and pepper.
7. Heat some olive oil in a saucepan over medium flame. Once it heats up, place chicken breasts on it and cook them for 5 minutes and flip them over carefully using a spatula. Cook for another 3 to 4 minutes and remove from flame.
8. Now place the chicken breasts on a baking tray and bake them for 10 more minutes.
9. Serve hot.

Creamy Buffalo Chicken Soup

Serves: 4

Ingredients

- 450 grams chicken thighs
- 115 grams cream cheese
- 3 tbsp. butter
- 80 ml hot sauce
- 1120 ml chicken broth
- 60 ml whole milk
- 120 ml heavy cream
- 1 tsp. salt
- ¼ tsp. ground black pepper
- 45 grams chopped celery
- 1 tbsp. blue cheese dressing
- Some chopped dill for garnishing
- Some water for boiling the chicken

Method

1. Add some water to a large pot and bring it to a boil. Insert the chicken and cover the lid. Cook the chicken until it turns slightly pink. Make sure you don't overdo it. Once done, drain out the excess water and place it on a cutting board. Shred it using two forks. You can also pressure cook the chicken breasts for 5 minutes and then give a natural release.
2. Combine some cream cheese, butter, cream, milk, hot sauce, chicken broth and salt, pepper in a blender and blend it until smooth.
3. Transfer this liquid to a saucepan and cook it on low heat. Do not bring it to a boil. Just cook until it starts thickening.
4. Now add the cooked chicken and stir all the ingredients using a large wooden spoon. Cook for another 5 to 7 minutes on medium heat. Crumble some blue cheese using your hands and add it to the soup. Cook for another minutes and remove from flame.
5. Transfer the soup to bowls, garnish with some chopped dill and serve hot.

Chicken Puttanesca

Serves: 4

Ingredients

- 4 large chicken breasts
- 2 onions, peeled and chopped
- 3 minced garlic cloves
- 1 tbsp. anchovy paste
- 1 can chopped tomatoes in tomato juice
- 180 grams cherry tomatoes
- 3 tbsp. black olives, pitted
- 3 tbsp. capers
- ¼ tsp. ground cinnamon
- ¾ tsp. sea salt
- ½ tsp. ground black pepper
- 2 tbsp. chopped parsley
- 1 tbsp. crushed red chilies
- 4 tbsp. olive oil or butter

Method

1. Clean the chicken breasts properly and pat it dry using paper towels. Using a sharp knife, trim the excess fat off them and season them with some salt and pepper. Place them in the refrigerator for 15 to 20 minutes. Remove from the fridge and allow them to come to room temperature.
2. Heat 3 tbsp. of olive oil or butter in a saucepan over medium flame. Place the chicken thighs on it and cook them from both sides until nice and brown. Set aside.
3. Add some vermouth to the pan to deglaze. This will help you scrape out any remaining bits of chicken that may have stuck at the bottom.
4. Add remaining olive oil to the same pan and add some minced garlic and onion to it. Sauté until they turn golden brown.
5. Add chopped tomatoes, ground cinnamon and cook for 2 to 3 minutes until they turn tender.
6. Add about ½ cup of water to the pan along with olives and capers. Bring this mixture to a boil.
7. Slide in the chicken breasts, sprinkle some crushed chilies and mix all the ingredients well using a large wooden spoon.
8. Cover the pan and cook for 20 minutes with the lid covered. Take the lid off and cook the chicken for 10 more minutes until the sauce is slightly thickened.
9. Garnish with some cherry tomatoes, chopped parsley and serve hot.

Green Chicken Enchilada Cauliflower Casserole

Serves: 4

Ingredients

- 560 grams fresh cauliflower head
- 110 grams cream cheese, softened
- 340 grams chicken boneless chicken thighs
- 110 grams salsa verde
- 1 tsp. sea salt
- ½ tsp. ground black pepper
- 100 grams cheddar cheese, grated
- 25 grams sour cream
- 1 tbsp. chopped cilantro
- Some water for boiling chicken

Method

1. Preheat the oven to 177 C.
2. Grease a baking dish with some cooking spray.
3. Wash the cauliflower head thoroughly under running water and separate the florets using your hands. Set aside.
4. Add some water to a large pot and bring it to a boil. Insert the chicken and cover the lid. Cook the chicken until it turns pink. Once done, drain out the excess water and place it on a cutting board. Shred it using two forks. You can also pressure cook the chicken breasts for 5 minutes and then give a natural release.
5. Once done, allow the chicken to cool off and cut it into chunks using a sharp knife.
6. Transfer the cauliflower florets to a microwave dish and cook for about 12 minutes.
7. IN a large bowl, combine the cooked chicken with cauliflower florets, salt, pepper, salsa verde, cheddar cheese and sour cream and mix well using a spoon.
8. Add this mixture to a baking tray and bake for about 10 minutes.
9. Garnish with some chopped cilantro on top and serve.

Spicy Chicken Club Lettuce Wraps

Serves: 4

Ingredients

- 4 small chicken breasts
- 180 grams grape tomatoes
- 2 tbsp. red chili paste
- 1 tsp. smoked paprika
- 2 tbsp. lemon juice
- 1 small avocado, sliced
- 4 slices of bacon
- 4 large iceberg lettuce leaves
- 2 tbsp. Dijon mustard
- 4 tbsp. sour cream
- ½ tsp. salt
- ¼ tsp. cayenne pepper
- 1 tbsp. olive oil or butter
- Some water for boiling chicken

Method

1. Melt some butter in a sauce pan over medium heat and add some bacon slices to it. Cook them from both sides for about 3 minutes until they are nice and crisp. Once done, transfer them to a chopping board and slice them up into strips.
2. Clean the chicken breasts properly and pat it dry using paper towels. Using a sharp knife, trim the excess fat off them.
3. Add some water to a large pot and bring it to a boil. Insert the chicken and cover the lid. Cook the chicken until it turns pink. Once done, drain out the excess water and place it on a cutting board. Slice them up into chunks using a knife.
4. Combine salt, pepper, chili paste, paprika, lemon juice, and mix well. Coat the chicken with this mixture and place in the refrigerator for 15 to 20 minutes. Remove from the fridge and allow it to come to room temperature.
5. In a bowl, combine Dijon mustard, sour cream and mix well. Add the chicken chunks to it and toss.
6. Wash the lettuce leaves and pat them dry.
7. Now fill each of these leaves with the chicken mixture. Add some tomatoes, avocado and bacon slices on top. Wrap the lettuce leaves and secure them using toothpicks.
8. Serve along with some hot sauce.

Garlicky Chicken in Cream Sauce

Serves: 4

Ingredients

- 4 large chicken breasts
- 5 tbsp. butter
- 1 tsp. garlic powder
- 1 tsp. onion powder
- 2 small white onions, sliced
- 3 minced garlic cloves
- 120 ml chicken broth
- 120 ml dry white wine
- 220 grams cream cheese
- 50 grams heavy cream
- 1 tsp. dried tarragon
- 2 tsp. herb mix (rosemary, thyme, oregano, basil)
- 1 tsp. weber Canadian chicken seasoning
- ¾ tsp. salt
- ¼ tsp. cayenne pepper
- Some raw salad for serving

Method

1. Preheat the oven to 226 F.
2. Grease a baking dish with some cooking spray.
3. Clean the chicken breasts properly and pat it dry using paper towels. Using a sharp knife, trim the excess fat off them and season them with some salt, garlic powder and pepper. Place them in the refrigerator for 15 to 20 minutes. Remove from the fridge and allow them to come to room temperature.
4. Melt about 2 tbsp. of butter in a saucepan over medium heat. Add some minced garlic, chopped onion and sauté until they turn completely brown. Remove in a bowl.
5. Add 2 tbsp. of butter in the same pan and let it melt over medium flame. IN a bowl, add some cream cheese and soften it using a spoon. Add wine, remaining butter and mix. Add this mixture to the pan and mix all the ingredients well using a large spoon.
6. Slowly add the cream while stirring the ingredients, followed by tarragon, herb mix,

seasoning and stir again. Add some chicken broth to the pan and let the mixture simmer until it thickens. Remove from flame.

7. Add the chicken to the baking dish. Sprinkle the onion mixture on top and pour the cream mixture over it.
8. Bake in the oven for 45 minutes until it is completely cooked.
9. Serve along with raw salad.

Chapter 10: Meat Recipes

Bacon Cabbage Beef Stew

Serves: 4

Ingredients

- 225 grams organic bacon
- 1120 grams grass fed chuck roast
- 2 large red onion, finely chopped
- 1 tsp. minced garlic
- 1 small cabbage head
- 1 tsp. kosher salt
- ½ tsp. ground black pepper
- 1 sprig of thyme
- 240 ml beef broth, homemade
- 2 tbsp. lemon juice
- 2 tbsp. olive oil
- 1 tsp. chili flakes

Method

1. Pat the bacon dry and place it on a cutting board. Slice it up into pieces using a kitchen knife.
2. Similarly, pat the beef dry using paper towels and trim the excess fat off using a knife. Season the beef with lots of salt and pepper and let it rest in the fridge for about 45 minutes. Don't forget to bring the beef to room temperature before you start cooking.
3. Heat one-tbsp. olive oil in a saucepan over medium flame. Add the bacon slices and fry them for about 2 minutes on each side until they are slightly browned. Remove them on a paper towel.
4. Add the remaining olive oil in the same pan and add minced garlic and onion. Sauté them until completely golden brown. Keep stirring them often to avoid burning.
5. Add the chuck roast and cook it from all sides by flipping them over after every 3 minutes. Make sure that the roast is completely browned but not burnt.
6. Chop the cabbage into thin slices and add it to the pan.
7. Slide in the bacon, pour some beef broth, sprinkle some chili flakes and let the stew cook on low heat for 7 hours. You can also cook this stew in a slow cooker.
8. Once done, drizzle some lemon juice and stir.
9. Crush the thyme sprig in between your palms.
10. Garnish the stew with them and serve hot.

Bacon Cheese Burger Meatloaf

Serves: 6

Ingredients

For the meatloaf

- 450 grams bacon
- 450 grams ground beef
- 450 grams ground pork
- 180 grams button mushrooms, diced
- 90 grams dill
- 2 tbsp. yellow mustard
- 2 tbsp. spicy brown mustard
- 1 tsp. minced garlic
- 120 grams almond flour
- 1 tsp. garlic powder
- 1 tsp. sea salt
- ½ tsp. ground black pepper
- 1 large egg

For caramelized onions

- 2 large yellow onions, thinly sliced
- ¼ tsp. salt

For the garnish

- 100 grams smoked cheese sauce for garnish
- 2 jalapenos, thinly sliced
- Some chopped cilantro

Method

1. Preheat the oven to 177 C.
2. Grease a baking dish with some oil.
3. Place an aluminum foil on the wire rack.
4. Add the bacon on top and bake for about 15 minutes until nice and crispy. Remove the bacon on paper towels. Preserve the remaining bacon fat for caramelizing the onions.
5. In a large bowl, add the ground beef, pork, bell pepper, onion, garlic powder, minced garlic, almond flour, mushrooms, dill, yellow mustard, brown mustard, salt,

egg and mix well using a spoon or a spatula. You can also use an electric beater to mix all the ingredients. I generally use my hands to mix the ingredients and form a nice dough.

6. Add this mixture to a baking dish and bake for 70 minutes until completely cooked.

7. In the meanwhile, add the remaining bacon fat to a saucepan and allow it to heat up. Add sliced onion, some salt and fry them for about 20 to 25 minutes until they are completely caramelized. A good trick to avoid burning the onions is to cook them on slow flame.

8. Once the meatloaf is baked, allow it to cool down for about 20 minutes and transfer it to a large serving dish.

9. Add some smoked cheese on top of the meatloaf, caramelized onion, sliced jalapenos, some cilantro and serve immediately.

Keto Crispy Sesame Beef

Serves: 4

Ingredients

- 1 medium radish
- 450 grams rib eye steak
- 1 tbsp. coconut flour
- 1 tbsp. coconut oil
- 4 tbsp. soy sauce
- ½ tsp. guar gum
- 1 tsp. sesame oil
- 1 tsp. oyster sauce
- 2 tbsp. rice wine vinegar
- 1 tsp. sriracha sauce
- 1 tsp. red pepper flakes
- 1 tbsp. toasted sesame seeds
- 1 small red bell pepper, thinly sliced
- 1 small jalapeno pepper, sliced
- 1 small green onion, finely chopped
- 1 tsp. minced garlic clove
- 1 tsp. minced ginger
- 7 drops of stevia
- Some oil for frying

Method

1. Begin by washing the radish thoroughly under some running water. Pat it dry and peel the skin off using a peeler. Now using a spiralizer, slice the radish into noodle like strings and soak it in a bowl filled with cold water for 20 minutes.
2. Place the rib eye steaks on a cutting board and cut them into thick strips using a sharp knife. Add the strips to a bowl, sprinkle some coconut flour and guar gum on it and mix. The flour will bind the mixture properly. Let it rest for 10 minutes.
3. Heat some oil in a large skillet and let it heat up on medium flame. To this, add some minced ginger, garlic and fry for 2 minutes until they turn slightly brown. Add peppers and cook for another minute until tender.
4. Drizzle some oyster sauce, soy sauce, vinegar, sesame seeds, stevia, and sriracha and mix well using a spoon. Cook for about 2 minutes while stirring continuously.
5. Add some sesame oil to another pan and heat it over medium flame. Now add the

rib eye strips and fry for about 3 minutes on each side until they start turning slightly brown.

6. Now transfer these strips to the sauce and cook for 3 minutes until slightly thick.
7. Transfer the beef on a large plate.
8. Add the radish noodles on top along with some jalapeno slices and green onion.
9. Serve hot.

Thai BBQ Pork Salad

Serves: 4

Ingredients:

<u>For the salad:</u>

- 570 grams pork, cooked, pulled
- 90 grams fresh cilantro, chopped
- 720 grams romaine lettuce
- 1 medium red bell pepper, chopped

<u>For the Thai BBQ sauce:</u>

- 4 tbsp. tomato paste
- 2 tsp. creamy peanut butter
- Zest of 1 lime
- Juice of 1 lime
- 2 tsp. red curry paste
- ½ tsp. red pepper flakes
- 20 drops liquid stevia
- 5-6 tbsp. soy sauce or coconut aminos
- 45 grams fresh cilantro, chopped
- 2 tsp. five spice powder
- 3 tbsp. rice wine vinegar
- 2 tsp. fish sauce
- 1 tsp. mango extract

Method:

1. To make sauce: Whisk together all the ingredients of the sauce in a bowl and set aside for a while for the flavors to set in.
2. Mix together in a bowl, lettuce, cilantro and red bell pepper.
3. Divide among 4 plates. Divide and place the pork over it. Pour sauce over the pork and serve.

Garlic Mascarpone Broccoli Alfredo Fried Pizza

Serves: 8

Ingredients:

- 2 tbsp. garlic olive oil
- 200 grams mozzarella cheese, shredded
- 200 grams pizza cheese blend, shredded
- 50 grams Asiago cheese or to taste, shaved
- 50 grams mascarpone cheese
- 2 tbsp. heavy cream
- 120 grams broccoli, chopped, steamed
- 4 tbsp. ghee
- 2 tsp. garlic, minced
- ¼ tsp. lemon pepper seasoning
- ¼ tsp. salt or to taste

Method:

1. Place a nonstick pan over medium heat. Add oil. When the oil is heated, add pizza cheese blend and spread it all over to form a round.
2. Once it spreads, do not stir. Cook until it begins to brown around the edges.
3. Gently try to slide from the edges towards the middle with a silicone spatula. Slide it on to a plate.
4. Add ghee, cream, mascarpone cheese, lemon pepper, garlic and salt into the pan.
5. Place the pan over medium heat. When the mixture begins to bubble, remove from heat.
6. Pour half the mixture over the cheese crust and spread it.
7. Add remaining cheese mixture and broccoli into a pan and place the pan over medium heat. Heat for a minute.
8. Spread the broccoli over the pizza crust. Sprinkle Asiago cheese over it and serve.

Easy Keto Lasagna

Serves: 6 to 7

Ingredients

- 450 grams Italian sausages
- 340 grams ground beef
- ½ yellow onion, sliced
- 1 tsp. minced garlic
- 480 ml marinara sauce
- 450 grams ricotta cheese
- 1 large egg
- ½ tsp. salt
- 340 grams mozzarella cheese, sliced
- 75 grams parmesan cheese, shredded
- 450 grams chicken breast, boneless

Method

1. Preheat the oven to 215 C
2. Grease a baking tray using some cooking oil or butter.
3. Place the Italian sausages on a cutting board and slice them up into small pieces.
4. Add them to a bowl along with some ground beef, onion, and marinara sauce, garlic and mix well.
5. Heat a saucepan over medium flame and add the sauce to it. Cook it for 5 to 6 minutes on low flame until it starts thickening.
6. In the meanwhile, add some ricotta cheese to a bowl along with some salt. Crack an egg into the bowl and mix well using a fork.
7. Pat the chicken breasts dry using paper towels and trim the excess fat off. Slice it up using a sharp knife. Season it with some salt and set aside for 5 minutes.
8. Place the chicken breast slices on the baking dish and pour the beef sauce on top.
9. Now spread some ricotta cheese mixture on top and spread it evenly using a spatula.
10. Add some Parmesan cheese and repeat the layers of cheese turn by turn.
11. Cover the baking dish with a foil but ensure that it does not touch the lasagna.
12. Bake in the oven for 25 minutes until the cheese is golden brown.
13. Let it cool off for 15 minutes and serve.

Pizza with Sausages

Serves: 6

Ingredients

- 2 tbsp. olive oil
- 1 cauliflower head (trim and then chop the head into smaller pieces)
- 30 grams white onion (minced)
- 3 tbsp. butter
- ½ cup water
- 4 eggs (2 large eggs)
- 300 grams mozzarella cheese (shredded and chopped into smaller pieces)
- 2 tsp. fennel seeds
- 3 tsp. Italian seasoning
- 50 grams parmesan (grated)
- 150 ml Pizza Sauce (pick a sauce that is very low in carbohydrates)
- 450 grams Italian sausage (look for the sausage that has a very low amount of carbohydrates)
- 100 grams Italian cheese (preferably get the five cheese blend. You will have to shred the cheese.)

Method

For the crust

1. Preheat the oven to 205 C.
2. Take a cookie sheet and grease it well with the olive oil.
3. Take a large skillet and place it on a medium flame.
4. Add the butter to the skillet and add the onions to the skillet and sauté them until they are translucent. Add the cauliflower to the skillet and cook it until it is almost done.
5. Add water to the skillet and cover the skillet. Leave the vegetables in until the cauliflower is cooked and soft.
6. Transfer the vegetables to a glass bowl and leave them to cool.
7. As the cauliflower is cooling, you will need to cook the Italian sausages. You will need to break them into smaller pieces and cook them well. Drain all the fat out from the skillet. Pat the sausages dry on a tissue paper to remove any excess fat.

Leave these aside to cool.

8. Once the cauliflower has cooled down, take three cups of the cauliflower and place it in a food processor or a blender. You will need to blend it until the cauliflower has turned into a smooth puree. Move the puree into a mixing bowl.

9. Add the eggs to the mixing bowl along with the cheese and the spices. Blend them well. Now add the Parmesan cheese and mix it well!

10. Add the cauliflower puree to the cookie sheet and spread it neatly with a spatula. You will have to have a certain thickness all around the sheet.

11. Bake the crust in the oven for twenty minutes. Remove the crust when you find that it has turned brown at the edges.

12. While the pizza crust is in the oven, you will need to chop the sausages into fine pieces. You could either cut the sausage or process it in the food processor.

13. Pour the pizza sauce in a saucepan and add the Italian sausage to the pan.

14. Cook the sausage in the pizza sauce until the sauce has become thick.

For the pizza

1. Once the crust is cooked, you can remove it from the oven and turn the oven settings to boil. Leave the oven shelf four inches from the broiler.

2. Pour the sausage and sauce mixture over the crust. Spread the mixture over the crust using a spatula. You will have a thin coating of the sauce and the sausage. You could add more sausage and sauce to the crust if you want.

3. Leave the pizza in the oven and broil it until the cheese melts. You have to ensure that the cheese has begun to bubble.

4. Remove the pizza from the oven and cut how many ever slices you want.

Keto Style Moroccan Meatballs

Serves: 4

Ingredients

- 450 grams ground lamb
- 2 tsp. freshly chopped coriander
- 1 tsp. minced garlic
- 1 tsp. ground coriander
- 2 tbsp. finely chopped mint
- ½ tsp. onion powder
- ¼ tsp. oregano
- 2 tsp. thyme
- Zest of one lemon
- 60 ml coconut milk, full fat
- 1 tsp. lemon juice
- ½ tsp. allspice powder
- ¼ tsp. ground black pepper
- ¼ tsp. curry powder
- 1 tsp. kosher salt
- ¼ tsp. paprika
- 1 tsp. ground cumin

Method

1. Preheat the oven to 177 C.
2. Grease a baking tray using some cooking oil or butter.
3. Add the ground lamb to a large bowl and break it up using your hands or you can simply add it to a food processor and whisk a little.
4. To this, add minced garlic, ground coriander, ground cumin, salt, onion powder, allspice mix, paprika, curry powder, oregano, ground black pepper and mix well using your hands.
5. Once a dough is formed, roll out about 15 meatballs and place them on a foiled baking dish.
6. Bake them for about 15-20 minutes until they are nice and golden.
7. In the meanwhile, combine coconut cream, mint, cilantro, lemon zest, and lemon juice, salt and mix well. Keep it in the fridge until the meatballs are ready to serve.
8. Once baked, transfer the meatballs on a large plate. Insert a toothpick inside each of the meatball so it's easier to eat.
9. Serve the meatballs along with coconut sauce on the side.

Delicious Keto Coconut Lamb Curry

Serves: 4

Ingredients

- 4 tbsp. butter or ghee
- 680 grams lamb shoulder
- 1 onion, finely chopped
- 3 minced garlic cloves
- 1 tsp. minced ginger
- 1 red chili, slit
- 1 tsp. ground turmeric
- 1 tsp. curry powder
- Some curry leaves
- 180 grams chopped ripe tomatoes
- 480 ml beef stock
- 60 ml coconut cream
- 2 tbsp. chopped coriander
- 1 tsp. sea salt

Method

1. Clean the lamb and trim the excess fat off using a knife. Now place the lamb on a cutting board and slice it up into pieces.
2. Add two tbsp. of butter to a saucepan and let it heat up over medium flame. Add the lamb pieces and cook them from all sides until they are golden brown. Remove on a plate.
3. Add the remaining butter to the pan and add some minced garlic, ginger and onion. Sauté them while stirring continuously until golden brown.
4. Add some turmeric powder, curry leaves and let them splatter.
5. Slide in the chopped tomatoes, curry powder, slit chili and cook for 3 minutes until the tomatoes turn completely tender.
6. Now add the lamb slices, followed by some salt and mix all the ingredients well using a large wooden spoon.
7. Pour some beef stock into the pan and let it simmer for about 30 minutes with the lid covered until the lamb tenderizes.
8. Remove the lid, pour some coconut milk and cook for another 5 minutes until slightly thick.
9. Garnish with some chopped coriander and serve.

Curry Lamb Shanks

Serves: 2

Ingredients

- 2 large lamb shanks
- 3 tbsp. coconut oil
- 720 ml beef broth
- 3 minced garlic cloves
- 2 tsp. ground ginger
- 1 small onion, chopped
- 1 tsp. garam masala
- ½ tsp. chili powder
- ½ tsp. turmeric powder
- 1 tsp. coriander powder
- ½ tsp. ground cumin
- ¾ tsp. salt
- ¼ tsp. ground cinnamon
- 2 bay leaves
- Some lemon wedges for serving

Method

1. Clean the lamb shanks and trim the excess fat off using a knife.
2. Add 2 tbsp. coconut oil and spread it across the pan. Allow it to heat up for a minute and place the lamb shanks on it. Cook them for about 3 minutes on each side until they are nice and brown from the sides. Remove them on a plate.
10. Add the remaining coconut oil to the same pan and some minced garlic, ginger and onion. Sauté them while stirring continuously until golden brown.
3. Add some turmeric powder, garam masala, coriander powder, ground cumin, salt, chili powder, cinnamon powder, bay leaf and mix all the ingredients well using a big spoon. Cook for about a minute until the spices release their flavors.
4. Now add the shanks to the pan and toss.
5. Pour some beef broth and cover the lid of the pan. Let it cook for 10 to 12 minutes or more until all the liquid is absorbed.
6. Now place the shanks in a large baking tray and pour the remaining liquid on top.
7. Bake them for 20 minutes until they are completely done.
8. Serve along with some lemon wedges.

Tangy Lamb Meatballs with Mint Gremolata

Serves: 4

Ingredients

- 900 grams ground lamb
- 2 eggs
- 60 grams almond flour
- 1 tbsp. lemon rind
- 1 tbsp. lemon juice
- 1 minced garlic clove
- 1 ½ tbsp. Za'atar seasoning
- 1 tsp. kosher salt
- ½ tsp. ground pepper
- 3 tbsp. olive oil for frying.

For the mint Gremolata

- 2 tbsp. chopped parsley
- 2 tbsp. fresh mint
- 1 tbsp. lime zest
- 2 minced garlic cloves

Method

1. Add the ground lamb to a large bowl and break it up using your hands or you can simply add it to a food processor and whisk a little.
2. To this, add minced garlic, seasoning, salt, ground pepper, chopped parsley, lemon zest, lemon juice, almond flour and mix well using a spoon. Crack the eggs into the mixture and mix again using your hands while forming a slightly firm dough. Roll out about 20 to 22 meatballs with your hands. Set them aside.
3. Add some olive oil to a skillet and allow it to heat up over medium flame. Gently try to twist and turn the pan so the oil spreads all across it.
4. Add the meatballs to the pan and cook them from all sides while stirring them continuously until they are nice and brown.
5. In the meanwhile, combine all the ingredients for the Gremolata in a large bowl and mix them with a spoon. Add the Gremolata at the center of a large dish.
6. Place the meatballs on top of the Gremolata. Insert a toothpick inside each of the meatball so it's easier to eat.
7. Serve warm.

Creamy Mustard Lemon Pork Loin

Serves: 4

Ingredients

- 4 large pork loins
- 1 tsp. kosher salt
- ½ tsp. ground black pepper
- 1 tsp. paprika
- 1 tsp. thyme

For the mustard sauce

- 120 ml chicken broth
- 25 grams heavy cream
- 1 tsp. apple cider vinegar
- 1 tsp. lemon juice
- 1 tbsp. ground mustard
- Some green beans for serving
- 2 tbsp. olive oil

Method

1. Start by cleaning the pork loins and pat them dry using pepper towels. Now season them generously with some salt, pepper, paprika and thyme from all sides. Wrap them up with a thin plastic sheet and rest them in the fridge for about an hour. Bring the pork to room temperature before you start cooking.
2. Add some olive oil to a pan and let it heat up over medium flame. Spread the oil across the pan using a spoon or by simply twisting and turning the pan.
3. Place the pork chops on the pan and cook for about 3 minutes on each side until brown. Set them aside.
4. In the meanwhile, add some chicken broth to the pan and deglaze it. Add some apple cider vinegar, heavy cream and mix using a large spoon. Let it simmer for about 6 to 7 minutes until it thickens.
5. Add some lemon juice, mustard and stir again. Add the pork chops and cook for about 10 to 12 minutes until completely done.
6. Transfer on a large plate and serve along with some green beans on the side.

Slow Cooker Pulled Pork

Serves: 4

Ingredients

- 1500 grams pork shoulder
- 2 onions, sliced
- 4 minced garlic cloves
- 240 ml chicken stock
- 1 tbsp. liquid smoke
- 100 grams keto friendly BBQ sauce
- 1 tbsp. chili powder
- 1 tsp. salt
- ½ tsp. paprika
- ½ tsp. garlic powder
- ½ tsp. ground black pepper
- ½ tsp. ground cumin
- ¼ tsp. ground cinnamon
- 1 tbsp. olive oil
- ½ tsp. sweetener
- Some capers for garnish

Method

1. In a bowl, combine all the dry ingredients and mix them using a spoon.
2. Grab the pork shoulders and trim the excess fat off them. Pat them dry using paper towels and brush them with some olive oil. Now coat them generously with some spice mix by rubbing it all over them.
3. Heat the slow cooker on cooker on medium flame. Now lay the onion slices at the bottom of the cooker.
4. Place the pork shoulder on the onions and sprinkle some minced garlic on top.
5. Now pour the chicken stock and liquid smoke. Also add some sweetener on top.
6. Finally, pour the BBQ sauce on top and close the lid of the cooker.
7. Let the pork shoulders cook for about 8 hours on low or 4 hours on high.
8. Once done, allow the dish to cool down and transfer the pork shoulder to a large bowl. Now shred the pork using two forks. Drizzle the remaining sauce on top.
9. Garnish with some capers and serve.

Southwestern Keto Style Pork Stew

Serves: 4 to 5

Ingredients

- 450 grams pork shoulder
- 2 tsp. chili powder
- 2 tsp. cumin powder
- 1 tsp. minced garlic
- 1 tsp. salt
- ½ tsp. ground black pepper
- 1 tsp. paprika
- 1 tsp. oregano
- ¼ tsp. cinnamon
- 2 bay leaves
- 180 grams button mushrooms, diced
- 1 small jalapeno, sliced
- 1 small green bell pepper, sliced
- 1 small red bell pepper, sliced
- 1 tbsp. lemon juice
- 480 ml beef broth
- 480 ml chicken broth
- 60 ml dark coffee
- 50 grams thick tomato paste
- 1 tbsp. olive oil
- Some onion greens for serving

Method

1. Clean the pork shoulders and trim the excess fat off them. Pat them dry using paper towels and season them with salt and pepper. Set them aside for about 20 minutes. Later, slice them up into thick strips using a sharp knife.
2. Heat some olive oil in a slow cooker over medium flame.
3. Add minced garlic and sauté until it turns slightly brown. Add bay leaf, paprika, oregano, cumin powder, chili powder and cook for 30 seconds. Add some sliced onions, bell peppers and cook for a couple of minutes until tender.
4. Slide in the mushrooms and fry them for 2 minutes.
5. Pour some bone broth and chicken broth to the pan, followed by jalapeno chili, lemon juice tomato paste and stir all the ingredients well using a large wooden

spoon.

6. Add some strong coffee to the pan, slide in the pork and stir well.
7. Close the lid and cook the pork for 8 hours on low or 4 hours on high.
8. Once done. Transfer the stew in a large bowl.
9. Garnish with some onion greens and serve hot.

Orange and Ginger Duck Roast

Serves: 5

Ingredients

- 2200 grams duck
- 2 tbsp. kosher salt
- 1 tbsp. five spice powder
- 1 large orange
- 1 tbsp. grated ginger
- 1 tbsp. minced garlic
- For the glaze
- 2 cups orange juice
- 2 tbsp. honey
- 2 tbsp. soy sauce
- 1 tsp. thinly sliced ginger
- 3 star anise

Method

1. Start by rinsing the duck properly. Pat it dry using paper towels. Using a knife, remove the excess fat from the tail area and gently trim the flappy skin. Now prick the duck all over using the same knife. Just ensure that the knife doesn't penetrate it.
2. IN a bowl, combine the five-spice powder, salt and generously rub it all over the duck. Refrigerate the duck for 30 minutes and then allow it to come to room temperature.
3. Now zest the orange using a grater and add it to a bowl. To this, add some ginger, garlic and mix. Smear this mixture inside the duck's cavity. Place some oranges wedges inside and tie the legs using kitchen threads. Let it sit in the fridge overnight or for at least 6 hours.
4. Bring the duck to room temperature before cooking.
5. In the meanwhile, combine soy sauce, honey, orange juice, ginger, and star anise and add it to a saucepan. Let it cook for about 10 minutes until it thickens slightly.
6. Place the duck on a baking tray. Pour this syrup on top of the duck and bake for 40 minutes.
7. Let the duck cool down for 20 minutes and serve hot.

Chapter 11: Keto Appetizers

Bacon Poblano Hot Crab Dip

Serves: 6 to 8

Ingredients

- Ingredients
- 340 grams crab meat
- 8 thick bacon strips
- 220 grams cream cheese, softened
- 50 grams sour cream
- 50 grams mayo
- 2 small poblano pepper, sliced
- 4 green onions, minced
- 4 minced garlic cloves
- 2 tbsp. lemon juice
- 50 grams parmesan cheese shavings for mixing in
- 50 grams parmesan cheese for the topping
- ½ tsp. ground black pepper

Method

1. Preheat the oven to 177 C.
2. Grease a baking pan with some cooking spray.
3. Heat a saucepan over medium heat. Add the bacon and cook until brown and crisp from all sides. Remove on a paper towel. Reserve the fat too.
4. IN a bowl, add some cream cheese, mayo, and sour cream and beat with a hand mixer. To this, add green onion, poblano peppers, garlic, lemon juice, fried bacon, some Parmesan cheese and mix again on low.
5. Add some crabmeat and mix all the ingredients well using a spatula.
6. Transfer this mixture in a baking dish and sprinkle some ground pepper on top.
7. Bake for about 20 minutes until the top turns golden brown.
8. Garnish the dip with some more onion greens, Parmesan cheese and serve.

Spinach Mushroom & Feta Crust less Quiche

Serves: 3

Ingredients

- 115 grams button mushrooms, sliced
- 141 grams frozen spinach, thawed
- 1 clove garlic, minced
- 120 ml milk
- 2 large eggs, whisked
- 2 tbsp. parmesan, grated
- 50 grams feta cheese
- 25 grams mozzarella grated
- Salt & pepper to taste

Method:

1. Preheat the oven to 117 C. Press & remove the excess moisture from the spinach.
2. Place a non-stick skillet on medium heat and spray cooking spray over it. Add mushroom & garlic and sauté until gets fully cooked and become soft.
3. Grease a pie dish with cooking spray. Spread the spinach on the pie dish and layer it with sautéed mushrooms. Top it up with crumbled feta cheese.
4. Mix together Parmesan, milk and whisked eggs. Add pepper and stir.
5. Pour into the pie dish. Sprinkle mozzarella over it.
6. Place a baking sheet in the oven and put the pie dish over it and bake until golden brown.
7. Slice and serve.

Chicken and Zucchini Poppers

Serves: 5

Ingredients

- 450 grams ground chicken brisket
- 2 large zucchinis
- 3 green onions, finely chopped
- 4 tbsp. minced cilantro
- 1 tsp. minced garlic
- 1 tsp. salt
- ½ tsp. ground black pepper
- 4 tbsp. coconut oil or butter

Method

1. Wash the zucchinis properly and pat them dry. Now using a peeler, peel the skin off and grate the zucchinis.
2. Add them to a large bowl. To this, add ground chicken, minced garlic, salt, pepper, cilantro, minced green onions and mix well. The mixture may be quite wet. Do not try to form a dough. Just leave it aside for 15 minutes.
7. Drizzle some coconut on a large skillet and let it heat up. Spread the oil across the pan using a spoon or by simply twisting and turning the pan.
3. Using a spoon, add a tbsp. of the meatball scoop to the pan. Add 6 at a time and cook for 5 minutes on one side. Then flip over and cook for 4-5 minutes on the other side until its golden brown. Repeat this process with the remaining batter.
4. Alternatively, you can also bake these poppers in the oven for about 25 minutes at 375 F. If you wish you can also keep it under broiler for about 3 minutes until browned.
5. Serve warm.

Curry Shrimp Stuffed Mushrooms

Serves: about 15 to 20 mushrooms

Ingredients

- 340 grams white mushrooms
- 1 tsp. garlic salt
- 1 tsp. garlic powder
- 1 tsp. curry powder
- ¼ cup mayo
- ¼ cup sour cream
- 112 grams cream cheese
- 50 grams Mexican blend cheese, shredded
- 1 cup shrimp

Method

1. Preheat the oven to 117 C.
2. Grease a baking pan with some cooking spray.
3. Clean the shrimps and devein them. You will need to carefully remove the tail off.
4. Add some water to a vessel and bring it to a boil. Add the shrimps in it and cover with a lid. Cook for 2-3 minutes and remove from flame. Let it sit for 5 minutes and drain off the excess water.
5. Add the shrimps to a large bowl.
6. In another bowl, combine shredded cheese with cream cheese, mayo, sour cream, garlic powder, onion, salt and curry powder and mix well using a spoon. Add this mixture to the shrimps and toss well. Set it aside in the refrigerator for 30 minutes. Allow it to come to room temperature.
7. Now stuff each of the mushrooms with this mixture.
8. Place all the mushrooms on a baking tray and bake for 25 minutes until golden.
9. Serve immediately.

Bacon burritos

Servings: 2

Ingredients:

- 4 cups raw spinach
- ½ cup chopped shallots
- 6 slices bacon
- 2 tortillas
- 1 tbsp. butter

Method:

- First slice the bacon strips finely. Melt butter on a skillet placed on medium flame.
- Add the shallots and the bacon to the skillet. Sauté until the shallots have turned golden brown and are translucent.
- Now, add the spinach and cook until the leaves have wilted.
- Toss the ingredients.
- Transfer this mixture onto the tortilla and roll it.
- Serve with a mayonnaise dip.

Onion and Cheese Quiche

Serves: 6

Ingredients

- 300 grams Colby jack cheese (divide the cups of cheese into two halves)
- 1tbsp. butter (a little more to grease the pan)
- 110 grams finely chopped white onion
- 6 large eggs (organic or free range)
- 1 cup heavy cream
- ½ tsp. salt
- ½ tsp. black pepper (ground)
- 1tsp. thyme (dried)

Method

1. You will first have to preheat the oven to 300 degrees Celsius.
2. Take a skillet and place it on medium flame. Once the skillet has warmed, add the butter to the pan and melt. Once the butter has melted, add the vegetables to the skillet and cook. Once the onions are soft and translucent, remove the skillet and cool the vegetables down.
3. Take a quiche pan and grease it well. Add one half of the shredded cheese to the bottom of the pan.
4. Add half the vegetables to the pan. Make a clean layer of the cheese.
5. Crack the eggs in a large bowl and mix well. Add the spices and the cream and continue to whisk. Mix it well enough so that the mixture is frothy.
6. Add the egg mixture to the quiche pan and distribute it evenly over the cheese and the vegetables.
7. Bake the quiche for thirty minutes and pull the quiche out when it has set well and is lightly puffy and golden in the center.
8. Cut the quiche and refrigerate it. You can have the quiche thrice a week for breakfast.

Taco Bites

Serves: 6

Ingredients

- 1 tbsp. butter
- ½ yellow onion (chopped)
- 1.5 cloves garlic (minced)
- 225 grams beef (ground)
- 60 grams can green chilies
- 1 tsp. cumin (ground)
- 1tsp. chili powder
- ½ tsp. coriander (ground)
- 50 grams sour cream
- 100 grams Cheddar Cheese (grated)

Method

1. Preheat the oven to 117 C.
2. Take a medium skillet and place it on a medium flame. Add the butter to the skillet and wait until the butter melts.
3. Add the onions to the skillet and sauté. Make sure that they have become soft.
4. Add the beef to the skillet and cook until it is brown.
5. Add the spices to the skillet along with the green chilies from the pan and cook for five minutes.
6. Reduce the heat and add the cheese and the cream to the skillet and simmer for a few minutes.
7. Continue to stir the mixture for a few minutes until the cheese has melted and has mixed well into the beef.
8. Pre bake some piecrusts and add the mixture to the crusts.
9. Bake the crusts in the oven with the beef for a few minutes until the cheese is bubbling.

Chapter 12: Keto Snacks

Caramel chocolate chip muffin

Serves: 12

Ingredients

- 360 grams almond flour
- ¼ cup xylitol
- 1 tsp. baking soda
- 1 tsp. salt
- 1 tsp. Xanthan gum
- 3 large eggs (crack the eggs in a glass bowl and beat them lightly.)
- 150 grams cup sour cream
- 3 tbsp. butter (melt the butter.)
- 2 tsp. Stevia Glycerite
- 100 ml Caramel dip (ensure that you buy low carb)
- 150 ml Chocolate chips

Method

1. Preheat the oven to 150 C.
2. Line a muffin tray with paper liners or grease them well.
3. Take a medium bowl and add the xylitol, almond flour, baking soda, xanthan gum and salt and whisk them together.
4. Take a smaller bowl and add the eggs and beat them well. Add the butter, sour cream and the stevia Glycerite and mix well.
5. Add the egg mixture to the flour mixture. Stir well and ensure that the mixture is smooth and glossy.
6. Fill each cup with the mixture. Do not fill it up to the brim.
7. Leave the muffin tray in the oven for thirty minutes. Make sure that the muffins are brown and firm to touch.
8. Remove the muffins to cool. This will make it easier for you to remove them from the paper without too much pressure.
9. Store the muffins in an airtight container and leave them in the refrigerator.

Buffalo Keto Chicken Tenders

Serves: 4

Ingredients

- 450 grams chicken breast tenders
- 120 grams almond flour
- 1 large egg
- 2 tbsp. heavy cream
- 170 grams buffalo sauce
- ½ tsp. kosher salt
- ½ tsp. ground black pepper

Method

1. Preheat the oven to 177 C.
2. Grease a baking pan with some cooking spray.
3. Clean the chicken tenders properly and pat them dry. Season them with lots of salt and pepper and keep it aside for 15 minutes.
4. Spread the almond flour on a dish.
5. In a bowl, crack the egg and combine it with some heavy cream.
6. Now dip the chicken tenders into the egg mixture first and later in the flour. Place them one by one on a baking dish and set it inside the oven.
7. Bake for 30 minutes until golden brown. If they don't turn out to be as crispy as you want, you can broil them for 3 more minutes.

Smoked Zucchini Chips

Serves: 3

Ingredients:

- 3 medium zucchinis
- Salt to taste
- 2 tbsp. olive oil
- 3 tsp. smoked paprika
- Pepper powder to taste

Instructions:

1. Cut the zucchini into 1/4 inch thick slices, crosswise with a slicer or a knife.
2. Place the zucchini on a sieve in layers sprinkled with salt and pepper. Keep aside for an hour. Some moisture content of the zucchini will drain out.
3. Pat dry the zucchini slices with a paper towel and place on a greased baking tray.
4. Brush the top of the slices with oil. Sprinkle paprika and pepper.
5. Bake in a preheated oven at 250° F for 45 minutes. Turn off the oven and let the chips remain inside for an hour so that it remains crispy.
6. Transfer into airtight container when cooled.

Crabmeat bites

Servings: 4

Ingredients

- ½ can crab meat
- 115 grams cream cheese
- 25 grams cream
- ½ tbsp. lemon juice
- 1 tbsp. onion (finely chopped)
- 1 tbsp. red bell pepper (finely chopped)
- 1 tbsp. celery (finely chopped)
- 30 grams mustard (dry)
- ¼ tsp. salt

Method

1. Preheat the oven to 117 C.
2. Drain the crabmeat from the can and clean the meat well. Remove any bits of shell.
3. Make sure that the cream cheese is left to soften at the room temperature.
4. Take a large mixing bowl and add the ingredients to the bowl.
5. Bake miniature tarts in the oven. Add the crab mixture to the tarts and place them in the oven for ten minutes at 350 degrees F. Serve hot.

Easy Baked Cauliflower French Style

Serves: 3

Ingredients:

- 1 cauliflower
- 1 tsp. salt
- 2 garlic cloves, peeled
- 1 tsp. herbes de Provence
- 60 ml extra virgin olive oil

Method:

1. Blend garlic, herbs, salt and oil in a small mixer jar until it turns smooth paste.
2. Clean the cauliflower and cut the florets into thick slices.
3. Spread the florets on a large cookie sheet.
4. Apply garlic and oil cream on the florets.
5. Put in preheated oven to 205 C for 25 minutes. Turn the pieces when it gets golden brown and bake it until gets brown on the other side.
6. Serve hot with meats or chicken.

Cheddar Garlic Biscuits

Serves: 15

Ingredients

- 300 grams almond flour
- 340 grams Colby jack cheese (shredded)
- 10 tbsp. butter
- 450 grams cream cheese
- 4 large eggs or 6 medium eggs
- 4 tsp. garlic (granulated)
- 2 tsp. baking soda
- 2 tsp. Xanthan gum
- 2 tsp. sea salt

Method

1. Take a cookie sheet and grease it well. Line it with parchment paper if you do not want to grease it.
2. Then preheat the oven to 149 C degrees Fahrenheit.
3. Process the shredded cheese and one cup of the almond flour in a food processor until they have blended well and are granular. Keep this aside.
4. Take a large mixing bowl. Add the butter and the cream cheese to the bowl and place. You have to melt the better a little. Once it has melted, mix the butter and the cheese together. Make sure that the mixture is smooth and glossy.
5. Add the eggs to the mixture and continue to whisk. Make sure that the mixture is smooth and glossy.
6. Add the garlic, the Xanthan gum, baking soda and the salt to the mixture.
7. Add the remaining almond flour and cheese mixture to the egg mixture and whisk well.
8. Once the ingredients have blended well, add the almond flour that is left and continue to fold the mixture well. You have to ensure that the dough has formed.
9. Take a tbsp. and scoop the dough and place it on the cookie sheet. Keep the cookies one inch apart. If you want you could flatten the dough a little to ensure that you have a smooth biscuit.
10. Place the cookie sheet in the oven and bake for thirty minutes. You will need to leave the biscuits in until they have a golden brown color.
11. Remove the biscuits from the oven and cool to room temperature. You can serve it with a glass of milk.

Bullet Proof Hot Chocolate

Serves: one cup

Ingredients

- 120 mml water
- 120 ml coconut milk
- 2 tbsp. unsalted butter
- 1 tbsp. coconut oil
- 2 tbsp. unsweetened cocoa powder
- ¼ tsp. vanilla essence
- ¼ tsp. ground cinnamon
- 2 tsp. sukrin (optional)

Method

1. Add some coconut milk and water to a vessel and mix. Turn on the heat and bring it to a boil. Remove from heat.
2. Melt some butter in a saucepan over medium flame and add it to the coconut milk mixture. To this, add coconut oil, cocoa powder, and vanilla extract, ground cinnamon, sukrin and mix well. You can also use an electric hand beater to give this mixture a whisk until it is nice and frothy.
3. Pour into a large mug and enjoy.

Keto Banana Walnut Bread

Serves: about 10 servings

Ingredients

- 3 medium ripe bananas
- 240 grams almond flour
- 3 large eggs
- 60 grams walnuts
- 60 ml olive oil
- 1 tsp. baking soda
- 1 tbsp. coconut oil

Method

1. Start by preheating the oven to 117 C.
2. Grease the baking pan using some cooking spray or butter.
3. Peel the bananas and slice them up using a sharp knife. You can also add them to a bowl and mash them up using your hands. To this, add the eggs, olive oil, and coconut oil and whisk using an electric beater.
4. Now add the almond flour, baking soda and gently fold it in.
5. Transfer the batter into a baking tray and top it up with walnuts.
6. Bake for about 55 to 60 minutes until completely done.
7. Slice it up and serve along with some tea.

Blackberry Nuts Fat Bombs

Serves: about 12 servings

Ingredients

- 60 grams macadamia nuts
- 80 grams Neufchatel cheese
- 180 grams fresh blackberries
- 3 tbsp. mascarpone cheese
- 120 ml coconut oil
- 120 ml coconut butter
- ½ tsp. vanilla extract
- ½ tsp. lemon juice
- 2 drops of stevia for taste

Method

1. Start by preheating the oven to 177 C.
2. Grease the baking pan using some cooking spray or butter.
3. Place the macadamia nuts on the kitchen platform and slightly crush them using a pounder. Spread them evenly on the bottom of the baking tray and bake them for 7 minutes until crisp. Remove from the oven and allow them to cool off.
4. Add a layer of softened cream cheese on top of the walnut crust using a spoon.
5. In a bowl, combine some blackberries with mascarpone cheese, coconut butter, coconut oil, lemon juice, vanilla extract, sweetener and whisk until smooth. You can also use an electric hand beater for the same.
6. Add the batter on top of the crust and set inside the fridge for about 30 minutes.
7. Serve chilled.

Chapter 13: Conversion Chart

Reference Source: https://www.infoplease.com/science-health/weights-measures/us-metric-cooking-conversions

Measure	Equivalent
1 tbsp. (tbsp) =	3 tsp. (tsp)
$1/16$ cup =	1 tablespoon
$1/8$ cup =	2 tablespoons
$1/6$ cup =	2 tbsp. + 2 teaspoons
$1/4$ cup =	4 tablespoons
$1/3$ cup =	5 tbsp. + 1 teaspoon
$3/8$ cup =	6 tablespoons
$1/2$ cup =	8 tablespoons
$2/3$ cup =	10 tbsp. + 2 teaspoons
$3/4$ cup =	12 tablespoons
1 cup =	48 teaspoons
1 cup =	16 tablespoons
8 fluid ounces (fl oz) =	1 cup
1 pint (pt.) =	2 cups
1 quart (qtr.) =	2 pints
4 cups =	1 quart
1 gallon (gal) =	4 quarts
16 ounces (oz) =	1 pound (lb)

Metric to U.S.

Capacity		Weight	
1 milliliter	$^{1}/5$ teaspoon	1 gram	.035 ounce
5 ml	1 teaspoon	100 grams	3.5 ounces
15 ml	1 tablespoon	500 grams	1.10 pounds
100 ml	3.4 fluid oz	1 kilogram	2.205 pounds = 35 ounces
240 ml	1 cup		
1 liter	34 fluid oz = 4.2 cups = 2.1 pints = 1.06 quarts = 0.26 gallon		

Conclusion

Thank you once again for purchasing this book.

The Ketogenic diet might have sounded intimidating, but now that you know everything about it, it won't seem difficult. The ketogenic diet is not merely a diet but it's a healthier way of life. This diet will not only help you in shedding those extra kilos, but it's the key to a healthier life as well.

This book has provided you with all the information that you need to know about the Ketogenic diet, will help you get a better understanding of the foods that you can and cannot eat and the way in which they will facilitate fat loss. By adding a little bit of exercise to your daily routine, you will be able to lose more weight and your body will be more toned as well. You will feel more energized without having to depend on caffeine or any other stimulants. The added benefits of this diet are that your skin will start looking younger and clearer!

All the recipes that have been provided in this book are Keto friendly. Simply plan your meals in advance and get all the supplies you need. This will make following the diet much easier. So, all that is left for you to do is get started with this diet.

Thank you and all the best!

Made in the USA
San Bernardino, CA
18 October 2017